Asthma

Asthma

Carolyn Simpson

THE ROSEN PUBLISHING GROUP, INC./NEW YORK

616.2
Sim

18412

Published in 1995 by The Rosen Publishing Group, Inc.
29 East 21st Street, New York, NY 10010

First Edition

Manufactured in the United States of America

Library of Congress Cataloging-in-Publication Data

Simpson, Carolyn
    Coping with asthma / Carolyn Simpson.—1st ed.
        p.   cm.
    Includes bibliographical references and index.
    ISBN 0-8239-2069-0
    1. Asthma—Juvenile literature. [1. Asthma. 2. Diseases.]
I. Title.
RC591.S56   1995   94-25273
616.2'38—dc20   CIP
                                      AC

ABOUT THE AUTHOR ◇

Carolyn Simpson teaches psychology at Tulsa Junior College. She has a Bachelor's degree in Sociology and a Master's degree in Human Relations. In addition to teaching, she has worked as a clinical social worker and school counselor for eleven years.

Her daughter, Michal, was diagnosed with exercise-induced asthma in January, 1994. Since that time, Mrs. Simpson has involved herself in organizations designed to promote awareness of asthma and allergies.

Mrs. Simpson has written eight other books on health-related subjects. She lives with her husband and three children on the outskirts of Tulsa. Michal continues to play competitive soccer.

Acknowledgments

Many thanks to my friends and former students who took the time to fill out questionnaires for me: Marian Richmond Burr, Peggy Anderson, Sondra Shehab, Leah Hunt, Kristina Linton, Lin Drake, Elmer Ivy, Jamie Rolen, Alma Varner, Kathy Smith, R.N., and Sallie Clote. Special thanks to Sallie Clote and Norman Regional Hospital (Norman, Oklahoma) for all the asthma literature they sent me. Special thanks also to Kim Beebe for her information on allergies, and to Megan Beebe for sharing her allergy-shot adventures.

Last, but certainly not least: thank you, Michal, for letting me tell your story. Continuing to play soccer, you've shown that asthma is not the end of the world.

Contents

Introduction

Last July my daughter, Michal, attended soccer camp at the University of Tulsa. It was the hottest week of the year. The heat index hovered around 105 degrees, and the radio forecasts warned of ozone alerts several days in a row. Her dad and I watched her final camp game, played in the blistering morning heat. Michal was playing midfield, a position that requires almost nonstop running. Just before the half, Michal laced her hands behind her head and stopped running. She either had a sidestitch or couldn't catch her breath. An older player had shown her how to stretch her diaphragm like that to take in more air, but even I could see it wasn't helping.

By halftime Michal was wheezing and frantic. "Calm down," her dad told her. Dwain figured she was having an anxiety attack; I thought the heat was getting to her. After ten minutes or so, she did calm down and resumed playing at a slower pace.

By fall, we were seeing these "breathing episodes" more frequently during games. Someone once asked if she had asthma, and I said, "Good grief, no!" No one in our immediate families had asthma, and besides, Michal had had physical exams all her life and no doctor had ever raised the question of asthma.

In January I ran into a friend I hadn't seen since 1979. She had since become a grandmother of a little girl with asthma. She listened to my stories about Michal's "breathing problems" and said, "It sounds like asthma to me. You ought to have her checked out."

Well, to make a long story short, I did. And Michal was indeed found to have **exercise-induced asthma**. How ignorant I felt! The bronchodilator that was prescribed for her made much shorter work of the attacks than all the advice Dwain and I had been giving her.

I had thought only very sick kids got asthma. My kid was fine except for a few moments after a long run. Could she really have asthma?

Then I started to read, and the more I read, the more I saw that Michal was a perfect example of someone with asthma. She'd had allergies for the past several years, had had a lot of respiratory problems as a baby, and had a cough that wouldn't quit. When weather conditions conspired against her (like the heat last summer), her lungs went into spasm with the first long run downfield.

Asthma is the most common chronic children's disorder. Statistics indicate that 10 percent of all American children have asthma. Some say that between 10 and 15 million Americans seek medical help for asthma, and another 10 million rely on over-the-counter remedies. That's in one year!

Asthma can be life-threatening, as well as very mild. The bad news is that asthma is not curable. The good news is that it is treatable. You may always have to take certain precautions, but because of medical advances you don't have to lead a dull, sedentary life.

I wrote this book for people, like Michal, who have just learned that they have this mysterious, inherited disorder. But it is also for all the others (like Michal's siblings, Jaime and Jarrett) who don't have the disorder themselves but are affected by it nonetheless. After all, asthma changes families, not just individuals.

WHAT IS ASTHMA AND DO I HAVE IT?

CHAPTER 1

Description and
Symptoms

Asthma is characterized by wheezing, difficulty in breathing (shortness of breath), and increased mucus production in the throat and airways. That may sound simple enough, but it isn't. Some people with asthma wheeze; others cough and never wheeze. Some people with asthma can't quite catch their breath; others complain only of chest tightening. Whatever the asthmatic symptoms, the thing to remember is that asthma **comes and goes**. In other pulmonary diseases you feel these symptoms **all the time**, but in asthma the symptoms occur and eventually resolve (sometimes on their own). That's a big difference: Asthma is **episodic**.

HOW WE BREATHE

Before we look at what goes wrong in an asthmatic's lungs, let's consider what happens in an ordinary person's lungs. Dr. Paul Hannaway in *The Asthma Self-Help Book* compares a person's lungs and airways to an upside-down tree. Picture the trachea (windpipe) as the tree trunk. The two larger bronchial tubes that branch off to either lung are the tree's largest branches. The bronchioles, the offshoots of the bronchi within each lung, are the smaller branches of the tree. And finally, the alveoli (air sacs) are the leaves.

When we breathe, air enters through the nose, passes down the trachea, through the bronchi and bronchioles in the lungs, and eventually to the alveoli. Surrounding the alveoli are millions of capillaries, tiny blood vessels. Their job is to take oxygen out of the inhaled air and add it to the blood, which is then pumped back to the heart and to the rest of the body. At the same time, carbon dioxide is taken out of the blood and expelled. In order for us to live, the air has to make it through all these air passages and into the alveoli. Oxygen has to be added to the blood in the right amount, just as carbon dioxide has to be expelled.

The trachea is made up of bands of muscle. In a normal person's windpipe, the airway is unobstructed, with a minimal amount of mucus coating the sides. (All our bodies make mucus; its purpose is to catch particles from the air we breathe and move them along until we either cough them up or swallow them.)

AN ASTHMA ATTACK

In an asthmatic's lungs, the airways are supersensitive and easily made to constrict. (I'll go into the "Why" in Part II.) When an asthmatic's lungs start to react, the trachea does three things that make it so hard to breathe. First, the muscle tightens in the trachea (as well as in the bronchi and bronchioles), narrowing air passageways.

Then the sides of the trachea become inflamed and swollen (as tissue does in any inflammation). At the same time, the trachea starts overproducing mucus that coats the sides. Now, a cross section of the airway would show it narrowed from the muscle spasm, further compromised from the swelling on the sides, and filled with mucus, leaving little room for lifegiving air to get through. Sometimes, the mucus actually plugs up the opening. The wheezing you hear comes from forcing air around the obstructions. You can see why an asthmatic has so much trouble breathing. It's as if an invisible hand were reaching in and squeezing the windpipe shut.

ALLERGIES

Asthma is often provoked by allergies, but having allergies does not mean you'll get asthma. One of my daughter's best friends receives allergy shots once a week. She is especially allergic to dust, pollens, and molds. Without her shots, she'd have a runny nose, watery eyes, and sneezing attacks. As a little girl, she had almost constant ear infections, resulting from the allergies. But she doesn't have asthma. She breathes just fine, allergies and all.

Another friend has allergies, too, but her allergies provoke asthma attacks (in addition to the runny nose and watery eyes of hay fever). She takes allergy shots, not only to make her less reactive to pollens and dust and molds, but to keep her lungs from going into spasm at the same time.

I happen to be allergic to the sulfa drug Bactrim. When I first took the drug, my skin broke out in hives. Unfortunately, I didn't make the connection between the drug and the skin reaction, so I kept taking the pills. Within a short time I developed breathing problems. A quick call to my doctor confirmed my fear that I was having an allergic reaction to the medicine. In this case, the allergy produced a skin reaction: hives. The allergic reaction worsened because I kept taking the allergen. At that point, I began to have trouble breathing. I didn't have asthma; I was having a severe allergic reaction. If you have asthma, each successive encounter with an allergen will provoke breathing difficulties.

Many people with eczema (an allergic skin condition) and hay fever (allergic rhinitis) also have asthma, but you can have one without the other. If you already have hay fever, it will not necessarily develop into asthma, though the conditions are related.

WHAT ASTHMA IS NOT

Cystic Fibrosis

Patients with this disease suffer from continual lung infections. It is a permanent condition and as yet not curable. Because these patients produce too much mucus, they show many of the same symptoms as the asthmatic: difficulty breathing, wheezing, and coughing. But a simple sweat test (the person with cystic fibrosis produces too much salt) can show the difference.

Bronchitis

Patients with bronchitis have symptoms very similar to the asthmatic. They have inflamed bronchial tubes (because the infection is in the bronchi) and produce excessive mucus, which causes coughing, wheezing, and difficulty in breathing. But bronchitis is the result of an infection and is treated differently. It lasts until the infection clears—unlike asthma, which comes and goes.

Emphysema

This disease is quite different from asthma, and the prognosis is worse. The alveoli (which add the oxygen to the blood) slowly become destroyed. Like brain cells, the alveoli do not regenerate. Thus, the person with emphysema permanently loses the ability to exchange oxygen and carbon dioxide. Eventually, he gets out of breath with very little exertion. He is unable to climb stairs, run to catch a bus, or give a long speech. Asthma does **not** turn into emphysema; this is a disease particularly of smokers.

Pneumonia

Patients with pneumonia have many asthma symptoms. This is a lung inflammation that sparks a buildup of fluids in the airways. The result? Breathing difficulties. The patient wheezes and coughs for the duration of his bout. The treatment and prognosis differ. You see, pneumonia is something you can get over. Asthma is an ongoing, although episodic, condition that you **don't** get over.

Epiglottis Infection

The epiglottis is like a little cover to the trachea that keeps things swallowed from getting into the airways. (Did you ever start choking because "something went down the wrong way"? Well, the epiglottis hadn't quite shut when you swallowed that drink, and some got into your windpipe.) If a respiratory infection inflames the epiglottis, it causes swelling and sudden severe breathing problems. The patient with epiglottis inflammation is anxious (breathing difficulties usually cause panic), runs a fever, and drools uncontrollably. The condition improves once the underlying infection is treated.

Hay Fever

Allergic rhinitis can accompany asthma or be separate from it. The symptoms include a runny nose, nasal congestion, watery eyes, and itching of the ears, throat, and nose. (Hay fever has nothing to do with hay, and it is not necessarily accompanied by a fever.) When asthma is complicated by hay fever, it's useful to treat the symptoms of hay fever as diligently as the breathing difficulties. The excess drainage from nasal congestion only adds to airway inflammation. Asthma is better controlled when hay fever symptoms are treated.

WHO GETS ASTHMA?

People can develop asthma at any age. A family friend developed it in her sixties. Another was diagnosed as an eighteen-month-old baby. As young children, boys outnumber girls as asthmatics, but by adolescence the numbers even out. Girls often see an increase in symptoms after they've started menstruating, but for some reason, boys frequently outgrow their symptoms by adolescence. Let me rephrase that. Nobody really outgrows asthma. Some people seem to stop reacting to asthma triggers as they get older. Their asthma may seem to go away, but doctors have learned that it just as often comes back in later years. Asthma tends to run in families, but not necessarily in direct line. It jumps around. Uncles and nephews may have it; grandmothers may share it with granddaughters. As in Michal's case, cousins may have it in common. Having anyone in your family with asthma increases your chances of developing it. As you'll see in Part II, asthma seems to be an inherited condition.

SEVERITY OF ASTHMA

Although most people do not die from asthma, it **can be** a life-threatening condition. Recent statistics show that asthma contributes to 2,000 to 6,000 deaths annually in the U.S. alone. As a matter of fact, asthma deaths are inexplicably on the rise. Researchers think it's because people with asthma don't view their condition seriously enough and therefore delay treating their symptoms. If you wait too long to treat an asthma attack, your efforts may be too late. Given the medical advances in recent years, an asthma-related death today is needless.

CHECKLIST OF ASTHMA SYMPTOMS

Check any of the following conditions that describe you and then show this list to your doctor. Asthma is *not* a condition you diagnose on your own. A trained physician is needed to differentiate between similar conditions and especially to prescribe a treatment regimen.

- Wheezing (in reaction to exercise, stress, air irritants, or certain foods).
- Coughing attacks, especially after laughing or crying.
- Coughing attacks during the night that cause shortness of breath.

- Excessive mucus in your throat that you keep trying to clear.
- Difficulty in breathing, perceived as an inability to get enough air.
- Sensation of being under a blanket, breathing only stale air.
- Tightening of chest (as if someone were sitting on your chest).
- Breathing rapidly but not feeling you're getting much air.
- Tingling in fingers or legs because of oxygen depletion and hyperventilation.
- Avoidance of activities or places that cause you breathing difficulties.

CHAPTER ◇ 2

How the Diagnosis

Is Made

A qualified physician must diagnose asthma, not your best friend who may have the same symptoms, or a self-help book from the library. Just because you think you have asthma doesn't give you the knowledge to treat it. Television and magazine ads are always hawking some nonprescription product for your asthma symptoms, but these products are inherently very dangerous. For one thing, you could be treating the wrong condition. For another, these products usually contain a fixed amount of certain drugs. To get the right amount of one ingredient, you may end up with too much of the other ingredient. So save yourself the worry and expense by making an appointment with your primary-care doctor first. If you need to see a specialist, she can recommend one.

MEDICAL HISTORY

You can make it easier for your doctor. Know your symptoms, and find out in advance if anyone in your family has had any similar condition. It need not have been asthma necessarily. Any allergic conditions (hay fever, eczema, allergies) or respiratory problems are important to note.

When I took Michal to the doctor, I started out by saying, "I don't have asthma and no one in my family does. Her father doesn't have asthma, either. So there's no history there." I thought that about summed up her medical history. Little did I know that the doctor was interested in other factors. For example, did any of us have allergies or bronchial infections? Did Michal have many respiratory infections as a baby? Did she cough much at night? Did any distant family members have asthma?

Well, her father and I both have allergies, as does her brother and Michal herself. Her father has recurrent bronchial infections, sometimes resulting in pneumonia. Michal had one respiratory problem after another as a toddler and would cough nonstop no matter what cough medicine we gave her. And, now that I thought about it: two of her first cousins have asthma. Now the history was looking more serious . . .

Make sure (as far as you can) that you know the symptoms that provoke your breathing problems. Do they begin . . .

- after exercise?
- after being around animals?
- at certain times of the year—spring and fall?
- at night?
- after eating certain foods?

- during certain weather conditions: cold air, smog, humidity?
- after being around certain chemicals or fumes?

Furthermore, do you . . .

- have a history of respiratory problems (bronchial infections, bouts of pneumonia, hay fever symptoms, colds)?
- have a history of allergies?
- or did you cough a lot as a child?

PHYSICAL EXAM

The doctor will, of course, want to examine you, though there may not be much to note if you're not in the midst of an acute breathing episode. She'll check over your skin (for evidence of eczema, hives) and your eyes, ears, nose, and throat (for signs of infection, hay fever, or nasal polyps). She'll listen to your chest through her stethoscope, but the characteristic wheezing of asthma wouldn't be present unless you were having an attack right then and there. As a result, the physical exam often reveals very little helpful information.

The doctor will probably order a chest x-ray, not so much because the data will tell her you've got asthma, but because it could tell her if you had cystic fibrosis, pneumonia, heart disease, or chronic lung disease. Or even if you'd swallowed a foreign body and it was lodged in your throat. Even if you do have asthma, a chest x-ray taken between attacks will probably appear normal. So the doctor really wants the x-ray to determine what you *don't* have.

For people with nasal complications, the doctor may

order a sinus x-ray to determine the degree of nasal disease. It won't pinpoint asthma, but it will show if underlying nasal disease is complicating your asthma.

BLOOD TESTS

The doctor will also order blood tests. She needs to find ont about diabetes, because if you *do* have asthma, she must know that before prescribing medication. Second, a blood test can reveal your eosinophil count, which can tell her whether or not allergies are playing a part in your asthma symptoms. (Eosinophils are white blood cells that are attracted to inflamed sites and as such are hallmarks of asthma.) Three specific blood tests (called RAST, PRIST, and FAST) can measure the eosinophil count in reaction to specific allergens. These tests have problems: They're quite expensive; they take longer to get results, and they are less accurate than skin testing (described later in this chapter).

Other Tests

The doctor might take a nasal or sputum smear and examine it under the microscope looking for a high eosinophil count.

The doctor may also order a sweat test to rule out cystic fibrosis. You receive a very small electric current—enough to make you sweat. Then a monitor measures the sodium ions and chloride ions in your sweat to differentiate between asthma and cystic fibrosis. (The patient with cystic fibrosis produces more sodium than the asthmatic.)

PULMONARY FUNCTIONING TESTS

Usually, however, the most definitive tests are the pulmonary functioning tests. These tests measure your lung volume and how fast and how completely you can exhale. One set of tests won't indicate whether or not you have asthma; a second set (done after a breathing episode has been provoked, or after you've inhaled a bronchodilating drug if you were already in the midst of an attack) will diagnose the disease.

Pulmonary functioning tests come in a variety of forms. In the most basic one, you blow out as hard and as fast as you can into a gadget that looks like a breathing tube. It's called a spirometer, and it measures the force of your expulsion. Even though an asthma attack makes you feel as if you can't take in any air, what's really happening is that you're not able to breathe out much air and your lungs are filling up with stale air. The spirometer detects whether you're having trouble expelling air (but not what is causing the obstruction).

The distance you move the needle on the scale indicates how unobstructed your airway is. Your performance is compared to "Predicted Values" based on the performance of healthy people of your age, sex, race, and height. Obviously, a six-year-old boy is not expected to expel as much air as a twenty-year-old man.

You're considered "normal" if you can push the needle up into the green zone, which is between 80 and 120 percent of a person's best. Falling into the yellow or red zone indicates an obstruction and a breathing problem (or one about to begin).

Of course, you can have asthma but not be in the midst of a breathing episode. In that case, your spirometer performance may be normal. To get around that problem, the doctor gives you a second test after having provoked a breathing episode. Your results should be substantially lower.

If you're having a breathing episode, the doctor will administer a bronchodilating drug (you'll breathe it in) and then retest you. From those lowered test results (based on the suspected asthma attack) to your next set (after using the bronchodilator), you should see a 20 percent improvement in your performance. That 20 percent improvement (or the 20 percent decline once an attack is underway) indicates asthma. If airway obstruction can be reversed (as evidenced by the 20 percent improvement in testing), that in itself indicates asthma, which by definition is "reversible airway obstruction disease."

Of course, people don't always respond to a bronchodilator. Failure to improve by 20 percent does not necessarily mean that you don't have asthma. It might mean that you didn't use the bronchodilator correctly so the medication failed to reach the obstruction. It may also be that your problem affects the smaller airways; the bronchodilators only treat the larger airways. And finally, if mucus is plugging your airway, the bronchodilating medicine won't get past it to the inflamed area.

CHALLENGE TESTS

Provoking an asthma attack is a good way to determine airway hyperreactivity. The asthmatic's lungs, remember, are more prone to bronchospasm than the nonasthmatic's. If the doctor can witness an actual "breathing episode," she can know with more certainty whether you have asthma.

If you are scheduled for asthma provocation tests,

be sure you stop taking any asthma medication (nonprescription and otherwise) for at least twelve hours before the scheduled test. Don't drink anything containing caffeine (coffee, tea, soda, chocolate), as caffeine can act in ways similar to a bronchodilator. Give up smoking, too, for six hours before testing, as nicotine can cloud the testing results. Avoid exercise and air pollutants for two hours beforehand.

Types of Tests

Three different types of challenge tests have been designed to provoke an asthmatic reaction in susceptible people. The easiest test is to have the patient breathe in a neutral solution (in spray form) to which methacholine or histamine is added. Methacholine will induce bronchospasm in the asthmatic.

In the second test, the asthmatic who reacts to exercise or cold air is asked to exercise for eight minutes or breathe freezing air for five minutes. At that point, bronchospasm should be imminent.

The third type of challenge test is the most dangerous because the tester uses specific allergens or irritants to trigger an asthma attack. Since an allergic reaction can be potentially serious, these tests are done as a last step and with great caution.

ALLERGY SKIN TESTING

If your doctor suspects that an allergy is provoking your asthma, she may want to do more elaborate skin testing to determine the specific allergens. When we first moved to Oklahoma, my five-year-old son's face swelled up in a matter of hours to the point where he only had slits for eyes. We rushed him to the emergency room, where the doctors were baffled by his condition. "It's an allergy to *something*," they said, "but we don't know what; we'll need to run some blood tests." Jarrett wanted nothing to do with needles, blood analyzers, or skin punctures. His strength was admirable; his resistance was not. They finally gave him a steroid shot to reduce the inflammation and took a "wait and see" attitude. (Had he been a more compliant child, or had the reaction continued, they would have had to do the tests.) As it happened, whatever things Jarrett was allergic to, he became acclimated to; he has not had a similar reaction. Fortunately, he was not asthmatic in addition to being allergic.

If you have allergies that trigger asthma attacks, you'll need to know what the specific triggers are. Skin testing should pinpoint that. Three types of skin tests are done, and naturally the weaker tests are done first. The doctor wants to provoke a noticeable reaction (to identify the allergen), but she doesn't want to cause you cardiac arrest in the process.

The first test is the **prick** or **puncture test**. A little drop of allergen is placed on your skin, and then the doctor pricks your skin through the drop. If you're allergic, you'll have what's called "a wheal and flare reaction" at the site of the puncture. The raised area is "the wheal"; the reddened area around that is "the flare." A reaction usually occurs within thirty minutes after puncture. If you don't have a reaction, chances are your asthma symptoms are not provoked by that particular allergen. Your doctor will then move on to the next allergen.

The second test is the **scratch test**. In this case, the skin is scratched first, and then a drop of allergen is placed over the scratch. This test may draw a stronger reaction because more tissue is exposed. Again, the doctor watches for the typical wheal and flare reaction.

The last test is, of course, the most provocative. In the **intradermal test** a small amount of allergen is injected beneath the skin. Even though a very small needle is used, direct injection of the allergen can have a very powerful effect. Medication needs to be handy to counteract a severe allergic reaction.

THE FINAL DIAGNOSIS

In the final analysis, the doctor relies on her experience with asthma cases to help her diagnose your condition. Even then, she may not be entirely certain what triggers your bronchospasms, but she'll have a pretty good idea what can reverse those spasms.

She counts on you to provide her with accurate information. Covering up a drinking history or a drug habit won't change your condition, but it will confuse the picture. You need to be honest in answering **all** questions.

Because asthma is hard to diagnose when an episode is not in process, the doctor will run a variety of tests designed either to rule out something else or to pinpoint airway obstruction. They may be blood tests, a sputum analysis, chest x-rays, allergy tests, and most certainly pulmonary functioning tests.

Putting all this information together, including what the doctor observes about your demeanor and your appearance, she can make a reliable diagnosis of asthma. Not all asthmatics look or act the same, so more than anything else, a doctor's familiarity with the nuances of asthma is her strongest guide. And now, assuming she knows the trigger to your specific attacks, she can prescribe you some relief. For some people, it will mean avoiding the offending allergen; for most others, it will mean using medication to prevent or simply manage attacks.

PART ◇ II

WHAT CAUSES ASTHMA?

CHAPTER 3

Emotions vs.
Genetics

Perhaps you've heard that asthma is all in a person's head. In other words, there isn't anything **physically** wrong with the person; **his emotions** are causing his breathing problems. For example, take the kid who starts wheezing and gasping for air whenever his parents get into a fight. Or the girl who "has a spell" whenever she's made to take gym class. Do they create their own asthma attacks?

Myth has it that some people get so wound up in their emotions that they actually give themselves an asthma attack. In fact, I read about a woman who was dating a man her family didn't approve of. This woman had conflicting feelings about seeing him at all, and when she started sleeping with him at his apartment, she developed breathing problems. Everyone assumed her body was reacting to her family's disapproval. However, an astute doctor figured out the connection, not to her emotions, but to the stuffing in her boyfriend's pillow. She was allergic to the bedding! Getting him to buy new pillows took care of the attacks.

The point is that asthma is **not** all in one's head. No one can bring on an asthma attack unless he or she has asthma to begin with. There *is* a connection with emotions, as we shall see, but the **asthma comes first**. It seems that a person develops asthma and **then** develops psychological difficulties because of it. Imagine how you'd feel and act if you knew that at any moment you could suffocate. Is it any wonder that severely asthmatic kids lead sheltered lives, or that parents and siblings tend to overprotect them? Watching someone struggling for breath (and being powerless to help him) is almost worse than having the attack yourself. There's nothing you can do to help.

Scientists suspect there is an asthma gene. Some claim to have isolated one (though there may be more than one). If they could pinpoint the gene, they could use gene therapy to correct it. What they do know is that asthma seems to run in families, even though the line of transmission is not always direct. Asthma may skip a generation or jump around between siblings and cousins. Nonetheless, anyone born into a family with an asthmatic has a greater chance of becoming asthmatic himself. Researchers may not yet know which gene is the culprit, but there is good reason to believe that asthma is an inherited disorder. All of which is to say: You're born with the potential to develop asthma. It's either there from the beginning, or it's not. Of course, not everyone with the potential for asthma necessarily gets it. Circumstances have to be right (in other words, the triggers have to be there) to cause the person to develop the potential.

THE ASTHMATIC'S LUNGS

In Chapter 1 we talked about the role of the lungs in breathing and maintaining oxygen in the blood. The asthmatic's lungs and bronchial tubes are different from those of the nonasthmatic. His are far more sensitive to irritants, and when his bronchial tubes react, they constrict (squeeze shut). Let's look at some of the reasons.

Everyone with an intact immune system makes thousands of antibodies to defend himself against disease. But one group of antibodies (immunoglobulin E, or IgE for short) is actually harmful to the body. It probably protected primitive peoples from parasites, but it is not needed anymore. Nonetheless, the body still produces this antibody. If you're one of the many people who produce much IgE, you have probably developed an allergic condition such as hay fever, a food or drug allergy, or asthma.

Mast Cells

All people have what are called mast cells lining the walls of the skin, nose, intestines, and bronchial tubes. These mast cells contain granules of powerful chemicals, such as histamine. (**Histamine** is what causes the nasal congestion of hay fever, as well as the runny nose, watery eyes, and sneezing. People take an **antihistamine** to overcome those effects.)

The IgE antibody attaches itself to these mast cells. If you think of a mast cell (which contains the toxic chemicals) as a loaded gun, the IgE that attaches itself to the cell becomes the trigger. When some antigen (and for different people, it can be different things) is inhaled or swallowed and comes in contact with the IgE-bonded mast cell, the gun goes off. The mast cell releases its toxic chemicals, and the surrounding tissues become swollen and inflamed. White blood cells (eosinophils) are attracted and further inflame the area, increasing the mucus production. If you have more mast cells lining your nose, you'll probably end up sneezing. If more line your skin, you'll probably itch and get hives. If more mast cells line your lungs and bronchial tubes, you'll probably wheeze and develop asthma. The release of toxic chemicals by the mast cells is the reason behind an asthma attack. Preventing the mast cells from exploding is the intent of many of the asthma medications.

Beta Receptors

But first, a little more physiology. Our nervous system controls all our bodily functions. It's not a matter of your foot moving up and down; it's a matter of your brain telling your foot to move up or down. The sympathetic and parasympathetic systems comprise the nervous system, and together they act to keep the body in harmony. Most important signals are transmitted by these two systems. Pertaining to this discussion, the sympathetic nervous system acts to open or dilate the bronchial tubes, whereas the parasympathetic system acts to constrict.

The sympathetic nervous system has three types of receptors. (I bring up these details so you'll understand why certain medications work and others don't work for asthma.) The **alpha** receptors transmit impulses that increase the heart rate, constrict bronchial muscle, and increase production of mucus. If you remember what was said earlier about an asthma attack, you'll realize that constricting the bronchial tubes further and increasing mucus production would be the last two things you'd want to do in an asthma attack (where they have already occurred to some extent). So, obviously, you would not want to use any medication that would stimulate the alpha receptors during an asthma attack.

The **beta-1** receptors also increase the heart rate and blood pressure, so they would not be helpful to a person with heart disease. The **beta-2** receptors relax bronchial muscle and decrease mucus production, which of course, are your goals in an asthma attack. The problem for researchers has been to develop a drug that affected specifically the beta-2 receptors of the sympathetic system.

And why should the beta-2 receptors need bolstering? In 1968 scientists discovered that many people with asthma had either defective beta-2 receptors or an abnormal number of them. Since inadequate beta-2 receptors could not counteract the effects of a normal supply of the other receptors, the nervous system was not in harmony. This imbalance led to overstimulation by the parasympathetic nerves (which as you'll recall induces bronchoconstriction).

So the asthmatic is a person who probably has ineffective beta-2 receptors and an abundant supply of IgE antibodies. A high eosinophil count indicates mast cell explosion and subsequent inflammation (which is why doctors order those blood tests on your IgE or eosinophil count).

Asthma is a very real condition that originates in the body. As to what causes the mast cells to explode, that is the subject of the next several chapters. Again, it's different triggers for different people.

THE ROLE OF EMOTIONS

But to return to the subject of emotions, people don't actually **give themselves** asthma, but sometimes their emotions can precipitate an asthmatic attack. Any range of emotion can do it. Laughing is just as likely a trigger for some people as crying. A friend of mine in her fifties was recently diagnosed with asthma. Her attacks were often brought on from laughing too hard. She'd get to laughing, and then coughing, and the next thing she knew, she could hardly catch her breath. She also had trouble if she overexerted herself on a bike tour. For example, if she'd had to ride uphill against a strong wind, she'd get congested and start coughing. "Heaven help me if someone told me a joke at that point," she wrote me.

Anxious people are prone to hyperventilate. That means they get scared (for whatever reason) and start breathing too fast and too shallowly. That way, they are not getting any oxygenated air deep into their lungs, because they're huffing and puffing out air as fast as they suck it in. During times of stress, and particularly if you know you're subject to breathing difficulties, you may start breathing too fast. Hyperventilating can of itself induce an asthma attack, and hyperventilating **during an asthma attack** will most assuredly make it worse. So stress can cause us to act in unhealthy ways, which is why so many people think stress causes asthma. It doesn't, but it can make it worse.

If you have ever choked or been pushed under water, you know how panic only makes the situation worse. Have you ever dived into water and found you were somersaulting under the water instead of rising to the surface? The first time that happened to me, I thought I was going to drown right there in the YMCA pool. I got so panicky, I couldn't tell which direction was up. All I knew was I was running out of air. At the point I resigned myself to drowning, I suddenly rose straight to the surface. And then it occurred to me: I had relaxed, and the relaxing (versus the panicking) had led me to relief.

I know it's presumptuous to tell a person who's having trouble breathing to "just relax." But calming yourself, especially in the midst of an asthmatic attack, does help the bronchial tubes to relax as well. Tension leads to constriction, and that's the opposite of what you want during an attack. So even though relaxation techniques and psychotherapy seem to be addressing your emotions, remember that they are effective tools (along with medication) because your emotions **are** involved once asthma is detected.

CHAPTER 4

Allergens and Environmental Irritants

om and Sallie have been our friends for years. Tom has asthma and, among other things, is deathly allergic to cats. One weekend he and Sallie were going to be in town and needed a place to spend the night. My husband (but not at the time) offered to let them stay with him, even though he had a cat. Everyone figured it would be okay if Dwain kept the cat outside for the night.

Well, about two in the morning Sallie woke Dwain and told him they were leaving. Tom was in the living room gasping for air. It seems cat dander (flaking skin and saliva) lingers in the air much longer than other allergens. Even though the infamous cat was not in the vicinity, enough allergen remained to trigger Tom's asthma.

ALLERGIES

Allergy is the cause of hay fever and hives, and if you haven't guessed by now, it can cause many cases of asthma. In the lungs, where an abundance of mast cells line the bronchial tubes, an allergen (which is any allergy-causing substance) meets up with an IgE-bonded mast cell and causes the cell to erupt, spilling its toxic chemicals. The chemicals cause a bronchospasm, and the individual struggles for breath. Specifically, the walls lining the bronchial tubes swell from the inflammation, mucus production increases, and the tubes constrict.

There are three kinds of allergens: **contact allergens**, which have to come in contact with your skin to produce the reaction; **inhalant allergens**, which are carried through the air and breathed in; and **ingested allergens**, which have to be swallowed to produce a reaction. Allergies cause different reactions in people, depending on where most of their mast cells are located. Some people get a runny nose, watery eyes, and itchy throat; others get hives all over their body, and still others have a hard time breathing.

The actual process of developing an allergy has been explained. First, you have to be exposed to something (and you won't have the allergic reaction the first time you're exposed). At first exposure, your body becomes sensitized to the allergen (say, pollen, for example). Your body then produces IgE that attaches to the mast cells. The next time you inhale pollen, the IgE will set off the mast cell. Histamine, being one of the worst chemicals, causes an inflammation of the air passages in the lungs as well as increasing mucus and mucus plug production. And those reactions constitute an asthma attack.

AIRBORNE ALLERGENS

You can be allergic to an untold number of airborne particles. **Pollens** are notorious allergens. You can suspect pollens if your asthma attacks occur mostly during the pollination seasons: spring for trees, summer for grasses, and late summer and fall for ragweed. The worst possible circumstances are rain just before the pollination season begins and windy weather during pollination.

Molds are another airborne allergen. You don't necessarily see them or know they are around, but they can be found in moist environments: houseplants, water vaporizers, humidifiers, air conditioners, shower stalls and curtains, and in basements. Many people get even sicker once they start using a vaporizer for their congestion. How can that happen? Well, it's not that a vaporizer is inherently bad. It's just that you have to be sure to clean it after every use so that mold doesn't get a chance to grow again. Water just sitting around is an open invitation to mold spores. Some people who are sensitive to molds can't even have houseplants because the moist environment is too welcoming to molds.

Household dust is another airborne allergen. What actually is dust? Little bits of other potent allergens, like pollen, mold, food particles, mite feces and body parts, and animal dander. Animal dander is like human dandruff: the flaked-off parts of skin cells, not necessarily the animal's fur. It doesn't make much difference whether your pet is long-haired or sleek and furless; it's the dander that's the problem. Cat dander is the smallest of the inhaled allergens and therefore stays around the longest, long after the offending animal has left the premises. Cats provoke the most allergies, dogs next, and horses third.

Gross as it is to think about, **mites** are the major component of dust. Microscopic insects related to spiders, they're all over your house because they live off human skin. They don't carry diseases. But many people are allergic to these microscopic insects that live in carpets and mattresses. You can't vacuum them out either; they cling to the carpet fibers.

Sometimes **cockroaches** (or rather, dead parts of them and their feces) are part of dust. No one wants to admit living in a house with cockroaches, so many times a patient fails to realize that cockroaches are the ingredient in dust that is causing a reaction. Since doctors are sometimes embarrassed to suggest testing for cockroach sensitivity, the person never learns this information.

Feathers are also airborne allergens. Some people are so allergic that they can't sleep on goose-down pillows, but have to resort to foam-filled. If you find that most of your symptoms occur when you're in bed, you can suspect dust in the bedding or feathers to be the culprits.

Man has also added to the list of airborne irritants. Some people are bothered by certain cooking odors, paint sprays, chemical fumes, automobile exhaust fumes, and even colognes and high-priced perfumes. The soccer Team Mom of my daughter Jaime developed asthma after an allergic reaction to her perfume. She had been wearing the scent for years without incident. One day without warning, she started to wheeze and cough. Powders set some people off, including flour, which is a powdery substance. Another powerful irritant is formaldehyde, which is found in plywood and particle board and floor coverings. Obviously, people with negative reactions to any of these substances would find certain occupations off limits to them.

Even wood-burning stoves and fireplaces bother some people. A friend bought a house in Maine, looking forward to saving money by heating it with a wood-burning stove. Unfortunately the smoke brought on asthma attacks, and she and her husband had to spend a fortune using electric heat, instead.

Tobacco smoke is the most common airborne irritant— whether you're the smoker or passively breathing it in. Secondhand smoke is just as likely to provoke an attack. Since smoking is an addiction, it's very hard to quit, and it's equally hard for some people to ask others not to smoke in their presence. Too many people try to adapt to smoke in their environment, and their health suffers as a result. Several friends tell me that they make the smoker in the family go outside for smokes, as if that will keep their air pure. They don't seem to notice that their house still reeks of old smoke. It's in the smoker's clothes and hair, and it clings to curtains and draperies.

And last, **air pollution** bothers everybody, but especially the asthmatic or person with pulmonary disease. It was the air pollution over Tulsa (as much as the heat) last summer that provoked Michal's first recognizable asthma attack.

FOOD ALLERGENS

Food is a primary allergen for children. The worst offenders seem to be milk and egg proteins. Nuts and shellfish may continue to be a problem for people. The good news is that four out of five infants with food allergies eventually outgrow their conditions. The bad news is that for those who do **not** outgrow these allergies, their reactions can be life-threatening. Food allergies are considered mild when hives are the only symptoms. They're considered life-threatening if the reaction involves the lungs, heart, and blood vessels. This condition leads to **anaphylaxis**, which means the throat closes up; it is the most severe reaction you can have.

Food allergies are very real, and if you're unlucky enough to have one, you must never, never eat the offending food or anything in its food family. An allergy to nuts means peanut butter is out, too, and don't let anyone coax you into taking "just a tiny bit." One young man was allergic to peanuts. As a child he'd eaten some and almost died because his airways closed up. He had needed an emergency shot of adrenalin to reverse the reaction. With any food allergy, the first exposure results in sensitization; each subsequent exposure provokes a greater reaction. One evening this guy and his friends were out having cocktails. A bowl of peanuts sat on the table, and the young man wisely left them alone. When his friends offered him the nuts, he told them he was allergic to them.

"What happens if you eat one?" someone asked.

"My throat closes up and I can't breathe," he replied.

"You're kidding," the person said. "You couldn't keel over from just one little peanut."

"Want me to show you?" the guy asked, reaching for a peanut.

His girlfriend grabbed his arm. "You don't have to show us. You already said you're allergic to them."

"Nobody dies from eating one peanut," the friend said, clearly wanting the guy to pop one into his mouth.

Perhaps if the young man hadn't been drinking, he would have shown better judgment. Instead, he popped one peanut in his mouth. Almost instantly, his face reddened and he started to gasp. His friend thought he was acting. The young man had no adrenalin on him, and by the time people realized how serious the problem was, it was too late. Despite efforts to revive him, the young man died. Right there in the restaurant.

The moral of this true story? Food allergies are serious stuff. If you have any, respect them and make sure everyone around you understands as well. Make it clear you don't have a life to spare to show them what would happen.

Some people are allergic to certain drugs. Aspirin is a common problem for some. I happen to be allergic to Bactrim, a sulfa drug, so I learned to stay away from the stuff. But one time when Michal was little, I had to give her some liquid Bactrim for an infection. As I poured some in a spoon for her, I spilled a little on my hand. That's all it took for my hand to break out in hives.

Others are allergic to food additives, such as MSG used in a lot of Chinese food, and sulfites used to preserve foods.

OCCUPATIONAL ASTHMA

People who find themselves allergic to something in the workplace are said to have **occupational asthma**. Bakers might be allergic to flour, painters to paint fumes, secretaries to photocopying chemicals, and people who work in laundries to detergents.

Because so many chemicals are in use now, occupational asthma affects more and more people. If you find yourself having asthma symptoms only during the weekdays, especially between 8 and 5 (or the hours you work), you should suspect an irritant in your work environment. Remedying the situation may mean switching jobs or locations; more on that in a later chapter. Allergies account for a great many asthma attacks, but they don't explain them all. However, if you suspect allergies are contributing to your asthma symptoms, consider when your symptoms occur:

- At home in the bedroom (often sneezing when you make your bed)
- Around cats or dogs
- During the week (8 to 5 or working hours)
- During seasons when the pollen count is high
- When you use a vaporizer or humidifier
- Handling certain substances (paints and other chemicals)
- Eating certain foods, or eating in particular restaurants, especially Chinese.

If you suspect an allergen, you have a choice about what to do next. You can either avoid it altogether (which is often unrealistic), you can adapt to it (perhaps by using medications and/or taking allergy shots), or you can suffer . . . Just remember that the third alternative is not your only choice. (More on how to deal with allergens is given in Parts III and IV.)

CHAPTER ◇ 5

Viral Infections

Allergies don't explain all asthma cases. More often than not, underlying infections such as sinusitis are a constant trigger for asthma. If you consider that the nasal passages are connected to the throat and lower airways, the result should be obvious. Postnasal drip drains into the back of the throat and from there can enter the airways, especially when you're asleep.

The larynx usually keeps mucus from entering the airways, but when you sleep, the larynx relaxes, and mucus can then enter the bronchial tubes, provoking constriction. Many people who have asthma also have sinusitis or ear infections. The wise doctor checks for sinus disease and treats it as well as the asthma. If sinus problems complicate your asthma, no matter how well you keep the asthma under control, you'll always be a step behind if you're not treating the sinusitis as well. The sinus drainage (and possibility of infection) will keep triggering your asthma. How?

Your sinus cavities surround your nose. Mucus glands line the sinuses. Mucus is then pushed along into your nose by hair-like structures called **cilia**, and you eventually blow your nose to get rid of it. If mucus begins to build up, you can end up with a viral or bacterial infection.

Having an upper airway (or respiratory) problem can easily lead to a lower airway problem—one in your bronchial tubes.

You can easily recognize the signs of sinusitis. A headache right between the eyes is usually the first sign. Next are nasal congestion (or stuffiness) and plugged-up ears. Experience has taught me that when a pain reliever alone can't cure a headache, I need an antihistamine, too, as it's one of those tenacious sinus headaches. If your headaches and congestion go on for too long, you need to see your doctor. Chances are you have an infection that won't clear up without prescribed antibiotics.

Viruses are one of those things we have to endure without much medical intervention. The common cold is a viral infection. And as you well know, there's nothing much you can do for a cold except cover up the symptoms for the two weeks it's going to last. Most people survive the common cold without incident, but not so the asthmatic. Certain viruses may destroy the beta-2 receptors in the asthmatic.

In an earlier chapter, I described the importance of the sympathetic and parasympathetic nervous systems acting in harmony. When the beta-2 receptors are destroyed or rendered defective, the system is out of balance, and if the parasympathetic nerves prevail, the bronchial tubes constrict. Remember, it's the beta-2 receptors that promote dilation (opening up) of the bronchial tubes.

Small wonder that asthma often follows on the heels of a viral infection, and the symptoms clear up once the virus is gone. When people end up hospitalized for treatment of asthma, it's frequently because of a viral infection first. In fact, recent statistics show that 40 percent of all hospitalizations for childhood asthma stem from a viral infection.

Knowing that, you should always consult your doctor when you suspect an infection, because chances are your asthma will be harder to treat as a direct result of that infection. You will probably need to beef up your medication regimen (and you don't do that without consulting your doctor first!).

CHAPTER ◇ 6

Exercise-Induced

Asthma

I often wondered why Michal was able to play soccer for two years before we noticed the asthma symptoms. It wasn't until she started playing in the Under-14 league that we saw the problem. Now that I know more about asthma, the reason is clear. In the younger leagues, soccer is played in four fifteen-minute quarters. Usually more little kids play per team than in the older leagues. Michal played her first two years on the Under-12 team: Quickstep. She got to rest after each quarter, and because there were enough team members to sub for others, Michal (and her teammates) usually got to sit out a quarter. Michal also played a variety of positions, including her least favorite: defense.

In the Under-14 league, soccer occurs in two 35-minute halves. Twelve girls showed up to field the eleven positions, but by midseason injuries had dropped the number to ten girls. Michal regularly played forward, which meant sprinting downfield when the ball came her way. She ran for 35 minutes straight; there were no subs. And that's when we started routinely seeing the asthma attacks.

One episode was so clearly a result of her running that I can't figure out now why I didn't put it together. In one game, Michal received a pass and streaked downfield to the goal. She's not an incredibly fast runner, but her legs are long and so she can cover a lot of territory fast. At the last minute, she crossed the ball to the left wing, who then popped it in the goal. While everyone cheered, Michal grabbed her side and started to gasp for air. The ref offered to stop the game, but Michal recovered enough to keep playing. And here's the point. Many asthmatics have attacks about six to eight minutes after they begin exercising. But not all exercise is the same. **Running and continuous exertion are much harder on the asthmatic than swimming or less demanding sports.** Soccer is probably the worst sport you can play. Unfortunately, Michal fell in love with it.

The good news is that preventive medication and proper warmup can help you continue playing the sports you love. Michal played her last season with the help of a bronchodilator, and if anything, she played better because she didn't get those frightening breathing attacks.

Many asthmatics have what's called Exercise-Induced Asthma, or EIA, for short. Some asthmatics have only EIA; their asthma shows up only with exercising.

WEATHER CONDITIONS

Why should exercising set off an asthma attack? Some people think it has as much to do with weather conditions as with the exertion itself. When a person exercises hard, after about six to eight minutes he or she starts to breathe through the mouth. Now when you gulp in air through your mouth, especially in cold or windy weather, it goes directly to your airways, not having had a chance to get warmed through your nasal passages. Cold air is more likely to set off a bronchospasm, so when you mouth-breathe, you're not just stressing your lungs more, you're also irritating the airways with cold, harsh air. This seems to explain why Michal had more trouble this year in soccer, especially after a long run downfield.

Some people have a delayed reaction to exercising, but it's still EIA. They don't start coughing and wheezing until long after they've stopped exercising, and then the discomfort lasts for an hour or so. Most EIA attacks end of themselves within thirty to sixty minutes, even without medical help. Most attacks can be prevented or ameliorated, however, with some kind of medicine. EIA is the easiest kind of asthma to treat.

Hot and Humid Conditions

Some people don't seem to react as much to cold weather as they do to hot and humid conditions. Air pollution hovers over many large cities on days that are muggy and windless. The pollution, combined with the humidity, is enough to trigger some people's easily reactive bronchial tubes.

TYPES OF EXERCISE

As mentioned earlier, for most people it's the type of exercise that can cause the problem. Any activity calling for continuous running is too stressful. Soccer and long-distance running are examples. Other activities where the running is more sporadic are better, such as baseball (where you get to spend at least part of the time sitting in the dugout waiting to bat), or volleyball, in which there's more jumping than running. Swimming is supposed to be a good activity for the asthmatic, and I have several asthmatic friends who do well, even swimming competitively. Presumably, by swimming in a heated moist environment, you're not filling your lungs with harsh, cold air that can set off a bronchospasm. But for others, swimming presents different problems. Those prone to ear infections and sinus trouble won't be helped in this environment. Michal seems to react to the chemicals used in the neighborhood pool. She gets asthma attacks just swimming around slowly if the chemicals have recently been added to the pool. Of course, in that case, the asthma attack is probably an allergic reaction to the chemicals.

Avoidance of Strenuous Activities

Doctors suspect that EIA is underdiagnosed. Many people probably have it but never know for sure because they avoid any strenuous activities for fear of an attack. Even today, many kids shy away from those sports that have caused them shortness of breath. They may say the activities are "boring," but the truth probably has more to do with undiagnosed EIA.

A doctor friend was examining a patient for asthma.

"Do you have trouble playing sports?" the doctor asked.

"No, I don't play any," the young girl replied.

"Why not?" the doctor persisted.

"Oh, I've never gone in for that stuff," she said.

"And what stuff is that?"

"Well, I've never liked running kinds of things; I don't have any wind," the young girl said.

"When you did run, did you have trouble breathing?" the doctor asked.

"Well, yes," she said. "I'd get side stitches and I'd have to catch my breath a lot. So now I just don't play that kind of stuff."

This avoidance of strenuous activities is often a tipoff to a doctor that the patient may have EIA. Some people react to their breathing problems by avoiding anything likely to bring on a spasm. If they have EIA but never engage in any exercise, they may think (erroneously) that they don't have asthma. But since EIA is so easily treated (compared to other types of asthma), it's a shame to give up doing things that—with medication—you'd still be able to do.

Since Michal started carrying her inhaler to games, we've started noticing other players with the same hand-held devices. An acquaintance showed up at our sons' soccer game carrying an inhaler for her son.

"I didn't know he had asthma," I said.

"Well, it only shows up during soccer games," she said.

After that, I counted another six or seven players who regularly brought inhalers to their games. And they played with the same ferocity as their teammates. You'd never have known they had asthma unless you recognized the inhalers.

Prevalence of EIA

The bottom line is that exercise-induced asthma is not all that uncommon. Most people with asthma have it to some extent because aerobic activities work the lungs harder. Asthmatics, as you know, already have hypersensitive airways; anything can easily provoke a bronchospasm. Sometimes, it's a viral infection that sets trouble in motion, most often it's an allergen, but it's just as likely to be a hard workout and cold air that trigger the airways to spasm.

If you find yourself always short of breath or worse: gasping for air six to eight minutes after you've started working out, don't give up the sport necessarily. See your family doctor and determine if you have asthma (or maybe a heart condition). If you find yourself avoiding certain activities or locations because you don't like the way they make you feel, do the wise thing by finding out if it's asthma. Asthma can be treated, but you'll never find out if you just give up on activities.

PART III

TREATING ASTHMA

CHAPTER 7

What Kind of Doctor to See

Even if you're relying on an asthma book written by a famous doctor, *never* use the book to diagnose yourself. Asthma symptoms are often hard to differentiate from other pulmonary diseases and heart conditions, so you must see a doctor for the diagnosis. But what kind of doctor should you see?

THE PRIMARY-CARE PHYSICIAN

Nowadays, with insurance policies the way they are, the choice may already be made for you. Under many policies, you have to see your primary-care physician first. And that's a logical place to start. After all, specialists are more expensive, and you probably are not medically astute enough to know just which specialist you need.

So you make an appointment with your regular physician. He or she may be a family doctor or a pediatrician. Either is qualified to treat uncomplicated asthma. The only problem is that a primary-care doctor who sees all sorts of patients usually doesn't have time to keep abreast of all the developments in asthma research unless he has a special interest in asthma management.

If your doctor is uncomfortable managing your asthma case, he may refer you to a specialist. Your insurance policy will authorize payment if your primary-care physician recommends the specialist. Sometimes, it's only a short-term deal. The specialist may be needed only to advise your regular doctor about your treatment. You'll make one or two visits a year to the specialist and see your regular doctor the rest of the time.

The Asthma Specialist

Who is the asthma specialist? Depending on what is contributing to your asthma, you may be referred to a **pulmonary internist** or an **allergist**. The pulmonary internist is a doctor who first specializes in internal medicine, requiring at least three years of medical training *after* medical school. Then she'll spend another year or two subspecializing in pulmonary medicine, which deals with asthma, bronchitis, emphysema, and other pulmonary (lung) disorders.

The allergist is also an internist who spends one or two additional years subspecializing in allergic diseases. He or she treats asthma, eczema, hay fever, food allergies, and other allergic diseases. If your asthma is complicated by allergies, this specialist would be more helpful than the pulmonary internist. The allergist is able to devote more time to pinpointing your specific allergies and is more on top of latest strategies in treating allergies.

Good Points and Bad

There are good and bad points about specialists and primary-care physicians. The specialist naturally has spent more time learning about asthma and what new treatments are available. He or she has more experience with asthma because of seeing more of it in her practice.

But the drawback to the specialist is the good point about the primary-care doctor. You don't get to develop much of a relationship with the specialist. Once the asthma is under control, your regular doctor can take over. Some people are more comfortable with a doctor who knows all about them instead of having to pick up a chart and read who they are. Your primary-care physician (the family doctor or pediatrician) treats you for everything and over the years gets to know you pretty well. If you have a good relationship with your doctor (and you should if you mean to keep seeing him), you're more likely to call him when symptoms arise after hours. Chances are if you're regularly seeing your doctor, you're more likely to follow treatment orders, which means your asthma should be under better control. And if you do need to go to the emergency room for treatment, you'll probably receive more attention by having your own physician. A quick call to him from the emergency room should elicit his recommendations for treatment. And that makes the emergency-room doctor's job easier.

Honesty

One last thing about doctors. No matter which one you see (and that includes the emergency-room doctor), you **always need to be honest**. Being honest means telling everything about yourself that they need to know. Just because they don't ask you *this time* if you've been using pot doesn't mean that you don't have to volunteer the information. You must tell them your drug and alcohol history even if you know it will lead to a lecture. The same is true of smoking. Everyone knows by now that smoking is bad for the health, but withholding from the doctor the information that you smoke isn't going to change things. In fact, it can make it much worse when it comes to prescribing medication for you. Smoking and drinking can alter the speed with which your body processes an asthma drug. Being evasive or outright dishonest can have a direct effect on how quickly you recover from an asthma attack.

Changing Doctors

If you find that your doctor doesn't seem to know much about the latest asthma treatments, you might consider a second opinion. Even though it's difficult for a family practitioner to stay on top of all the developments, he or she should be willing to consider newer drugs and treatments. And you have the right to change doctors if you think yours is unwilling to substitute better treatments for less effective ones. Likewise, if your doctor doesn't seem to have much of a bedside manner, find one who does. You may have to accept brusqueness in a specialist. Sometimes it's a tradeoff: With a specialist, you're getting greater knowledge but less of a relationship. With your family doctor, however, you want someone who is easy to relate to. You'll be seeing him or her much of your life. It makes sense to *like* each other.

CHAPTER 8

Medications for Prevention and Management

I f you've watched television in the last few years, you've surely seen ads for several over-the-counter asthma drugs. Primatene Mist is one of them. Millions of people use these nonprescription drugs to manage their asthma attacks each year. After all, it saves them a trip to the doctor.

The problem with using such medications is that you're getting a mixture of ingredients. Some may be good for you, and some may give you unpleasant side effects. In the long run, you're better off seeing your doctor for a prescription tailored to your needs than taking something with questionable results. After all, if you're smart enough to recognize the symptoms of asthma, you should be smart enough to see a doctor about it.

cAMP

If you know a lot about science or physiology, you probably already know what I'm going to tell you about the chemical cyclic adenosine 3'5'-monophosphate (commonly known as cyclic AMP or cAMP). If you don't care to know all the details, I'll simplify the story.

When cAMP is present in cells of the lungs, it prevents bronchospasm. How? By preventing the mast cells from releasing their toxic chemicals, like histamine. So, naturally, cAMP is a good thing to have in abundance.

But there's always a bad guy lurking around. Phosphodiesterase is an enzyme that breaks down cAMP. If you have a lot of phosphodiesterase, you're not going to have much cAMP to help prevent bronchospasms.

Some asthma drugs, and theophylline is one of them, keep the enzyme phosphodiesterase from breaking down cAMP. Thus, the cAMP level remains high and effective against mast cell explosion.

THEOPHYLLINE

Theophylline is similar to caffeine in many respects, but more potent. One friend managed to keep her asthma under control by drinking a lot of coffee and tea. She was pregnant and didn't want to use asthma drugs if she could help it. Fortunately for her, the coffee seemed to keep the asthma symptoms under control.

Theophylline comes in a variety of forms. One is a short-acting oral medication that is taken every four hours, has its maximum effect after two hours, peaks after four hours, and is out of your body in four hours. The intermediate-acting drug is taken every eight hours, peaks after four hours, and is out of your body in eight hours.

Long-acting theophylline is taken once every 24 hours and may not reach its peak action for two to three days.

The following medications contain theophylline:

Aminophylline
Bronkodyl
Elixophyllin capsules
Elixophyllin – SR caps
Quibron – T divitabs
Slo-bid gyrocaps
Slo-phylline tablets
Sustaire
Theo-24
Theo-Dur tablets

These medications are taken regularly as prescribed. They are not effective when taken on an "as-needed" basis. They have to build up in your bloodstream.

Good Points

Theophylline products have several good points. For one thing, exact dosing is possible. Unlike some of the over-the-counter drugs with mixed ingredients, theophylline can be given in its pure form. It is also available in many forms: you can take it every four hours, eight hours, or in some cases, twenty-four hours. When dosing children, you can go for convenience over quick effects or vice versa. Speaking of children, theophylline comes in capsules, so you can break them open and mix the medicine with applesauce or chocolate pudding to disguise the taste. Finally, theophylline has little effect on the heart rate or blood pressure.

Drawbacks

The principal drawback to theophylline is that the effective dose is very close to the toxic dose. In other words, for theophylline to do its job, you have to take almost as much as the amount that would hurt you. Thus, theophylline has to be monitored carefully. Doctors do that through therapeutic blood level tests administered every so often. Serum blood level can tell how much theophylline is in your bloodstream, and the doctors can then modify your dose accordingly. Dosages vary according to your age, smoking habits, and diet. For example, drinking caffeine will increase your theophylline level; a high carbohydrate diet will do the same thing. The antibiotic erythromycin affects the theophylline level as well. Smokers use up theophylline faster than nonsmokers, so being honest with your doctor regarding your drug and smoking history is most relevant here. Disguising your smoking habits will cause the doctor to prescribe less theophylline than he would if he knew you were smoking.

Side Effects

Most medications have side effects. That's the price you pay for their aid. Some side effects are worth adjusting to; others are more troublesome, and still others indicate that you have reached a toxic level of the drug and need medical intervention. The mild side effects include nausea, shakiness, loss of appetite, and restlessness. More severe symptoms include stomach cramps, diarrhea, vomiting, severe headaches, and the possibility of seizures. If you experience any of the more severe symptoms, call your doctor right away. Chances are you've accidentally overdosed on theophylline.

Theophylline used to be the mainstay of asthma therapy. Nowadays, it's more often used as a backup to other drugs. It is useful in keeping asthma attacks under control, but it's often hard to maintain a therapeutic level. Also, the side effects are always greater in drugs you ingest because they affect more organs than just the lungs.

ADRENALINE AND ADRENALINE-LIKE DRUGS

Adrenaline or epinephrine helps to relieve acute asthma symptoms by opening the airways. It is given by injection (usually as emergency-room treatment for bad asthma attacks, bee stings, or food allergies). However, adrenaline is not for regular use. For one thing, it's injected. For another, it's too short-acting and affects both beta receptors; that is, it affects the heart as well as relaxing the airways.

Researchers started looking for a type of drug that would selectively affect only the beta-2 receptors, which as you'll recall relax the bronchial tubes and decrease mucus production.

First, they came up with a combination of theophylline and epinephrine. The problem was that both ingredients were in fixed amounts. To get a therapeutic dose of theophylline (and too small a dose wouldn't be effective), one often ended up with too big a dose of epinephrine. Definitely not a good thing for anyone with a heart condition.

And then they discovered the adrenaline-like medications: terbutaline and albuterol. These medications primarily affect the beta-2 receptors. (Remember, the beta-2 receptors relax smooth muscle (such as what lines the bronchial tubes), decrease mucus gland production, and slow the release of histamine from the mast cells, all without stimulating the heart.)

The advantage of these medications is that they're **inhaled**; you breathe them in, instead of swallowing a pill. They're known as bronchodilators because that's what they do: open up your bronchial tubes. Albuterol is the most commonly prescribed inhaler in the United States. It goes by the trade names of Ventolin and Proventil. Other bronchodilators are terbutaline (Brethaire), bitolterol (Tornalate), and pirbuterol (Maxair).

All of these drugs specifically affect the beta-2 receptors. They go by a variety of names: adrenaline-like drugs, bronchodilators, beta-stimulating drugs, and beta-agonists. The medications are not necessarily used on a regular basis; some are meant to be used only when facing an imminent attack. Some are used only before exercising or when around air pollution. But other people use their inhaler on **a daily basis**. A woman friend confessed that she skipped using her inhaler on days when she felt pretty good. But she soon discovered that her asthma would flare up when she started skipping doses. In her case, it was important to use her inhaler regularly whether she was feeling fine or not. After all, it was the regular use that kept her feeling fine. If you use an inhaler, be sure you know whether you're supposed to use it regularly or only when the need arises. And then follow the instructions.

Good and Bad Points

The good points of beta-agonist drugs are impressive. Because you inhale the medication, you send the relief directly to the source of the problem: the airways. There are fewer side effects because you're not swallowing the drug and sending it throughout your system. It is also fast-acting. Inhalers work within fifteen minutes, and medicine that's nebulized (like a vaporizer) can have soothing effects in even less time.

But there are drawbacks. Bronchodilating inhalers cost more. Also, you can come to depend too much on your inhaler, using it more often than recommended. That's dangerous for two reasons. First, if you need your inhaler more than every four hours, it means your asthma is getting out of control. You should be calling your doctor, not reaching for the inhaler. If you ignore this early warning sign, you may find yourself needing emergency-room treatment instead.

Second, if you overuse your inhaler, it can produce the opposite effect: constricting your bronchial tubes, rather than dilating them. Some people think if two squirts of inhaler make you feel good, then two more squirts will make you feel better. Of course, it doesn't work that way. It's like aspirin or Tylenol; two will do the job, so you don't take four or six.

HOW TO USE YOUR INHALER

Some people find using an inhaler tricky business. They end up spraying the medicine all over their face or only on their tongue, and neither of those places will help the bronchial tubes.

An inhaler is a hand-held device with a measured amount of medicine in each spray. That's why it's called a metered dose inhaler, or MDI, for short. Here are some simple directions:

1. Always shake the MDI well before using.
2. Take a deep breath and then let it out slowly.
3. **Hold the inhaler 2″ from your mouth.**

Open your mouth but **don't** press your lips
against it in any way!

4. Press down once to spray a dose in your mouth.
   Don't worry, the right amount of medicine will
   come out. Just be sure to keep the inhaler the
   required distance from your mouth. That, of course,
   is the tricky part, and it takes some practice.
5. Breathe in slowly and deeply; then hold your
   breath for ten seconds.
6. Breathe out slowly afterward. The idea is to de-
   liver as much of the medicine as possible deep
   into your bronchial tubes.

Many people—not just children, or the uncoordinated
—have trouble holding the MDI away from their mouth,
yet getting the medicine in at the same time. What helps
most is a "spacer." (Your doctor can prescribe one for you;
most cost about $21.)

The Spacer

The spacer is a cylinder or tube that attaches to the MDI.
You put your lips around the end of the spacer. The MDI
will still be the necessary 2″ away from your mouth, but
when you spray it, the medicine has time to break into
smaller particles before reaching your lungs.

It's hard to make a mistake using a spacer. You just
spray a dose and breathe in very slowly. If you inhale too
quickly, the spacer will make a whistling sound, telling
you you didn't do it right. The spray has a distinctive
taste, but it's not at all unpleasant. If you're supposed to
use two puffs (sprays), wait five minutes before repeating
the process.

The good thing about a spacer is that it makes the inhaling

mistakeproof. The drawback is that it's not very portable. When Michal is on the soccer field, she has her MDI and spacer in her bag, but during an attack she only has time to grab the MDI.

Sometimes, the benefits of the MDI may be psychological as well as real. Once during a game, Michal sprayed the medicine on her tongue but didn't have time to spray it again. She tossed the MDI back to me and continued to play. But she seemed to recover from her asthma attack. Later she told me, "You know, I don't think I got much of the medicine down my throat, but I ended up okay."

"Maybe the effects were psychological," I said.

"Well, that could be," Michal said.

I figured she probably didn't know what I was getting at. "Do you know what 'psychological' means?" I asked.

"Sure," Michal said. "It worked because I thought it would work."

Sometimes, particularly since asthma attacks worsen with anxiety, trusting that your inhaler will do the trick **will do the trick** before it actually has time to kick in.

Full or Empty?

There's not much worse than grabbing your inhaler in an asthma attack and discovering that it's empty. If you don't have a backup MDI (and you should always keep your prescriptions filled), you're in a bad spot. If you've ever used an inhaler, you know it's a little metal canister. How would you even know if one was getting empty? You can't see the stuff inside, and it's hard to tell by weighing it in your hand.

There's a simple way to tell if your inhaler is full or empty or somewhere in between. First make sure the cover is on the MDI, then drop it (gently) into a big bowl of water. If the inhaler sinks to the bottom, it's full. If it floats on the surface, it's empty or just about. The fuller it is, the lower it will sit in the water.

A drawback to an inhaled medication is that sometimes it is blocked by an obstruction, or it can't get to the smaller airways. Injectable medicine or oral medicine would be needed in that case.

Like theophylline, some of these medicines can be nebulized (put in a machine that turns the liquid into a fine mist). People who have trouble using the MDI, even with the spacer, can manage a nebulizer.

CROMOLYN SODIUM

Another drug, cromolyn sodium, marketed under the name Intal, is a good choice as a preventive measure. Cromolyn has been around since 1975, but doctors have been slow to switch over to it. This drug also works by preventing the mast cells from releasing their toxic chemicals. It works on both the inflammatory and late-phase response of an asthma attack, and it's the only drug to affect both.

In an asthma attack, you have the current problem that most bronchodilators will remedy. But then you're left with inflamed airways that are more susceptible to spasm the next time around. Cromolyn works to prevent the attack in the first place and then to repair the inflammation. It is also helpful for people with hay fever in addition to asthma.

Cromolyn, or Intal, got off to a bad start. Doctors are usually reluctant to try out a new medication on their patients, and the Intal device was particularly hard to master. It is now available as a nebulizing liquid and an inhaler. Cromolyn was also thought to treat only allergic asthma conditions, but studies have shown it to be effective in a number of asthma cases, including exercise-induced asthma.

Good and Bad Points

Cromlyn is extremely effective (if taken regularly) in preventing asthma attacks. Side effects are very rare, and mild at that. The most common complaints of throat irritation, hoarseness, and dry mouth can be relieved by using a beta-stimulating inhaler first before using the cromolyn.

The only drawback to cromolyn is that it does not stop an asthma attack once it's begun. It is only preventive, so of course, you need to use the medicine regularly to control chronic asthma.

Someone relying on the adrenaline-like drugs would use them to prevent an asthma attack as well as to reverse one. Michal takes two puffs of her Ventolin inhaler fifteen minutes before games. If she still gets an attack during the game, she takes another two puffs. With Intal, on the other hand, you could use it before exercise (or on a regular basis), but if you had an attack during a game you'd have to use an adrenaline-like drug to stop it.

Combined with a beta-stimulating drug (such as albuterol), cromolyn is very effective in controlling mild to moderate asthma conditions. If your asthma is severe and your airways are chronically inflamed, you may have to resort to heavier-duty medications.

CHAPTER 9

Medications for Chronic or Severe Asthma

You've no doubt heard about the dangers of using anabolic steroids. Athletes have used these drugs to improve muscle mass, only to find out later that the drugs cause serious side effects. Doctors originally prescribed anabolic steroids to repair muscle injury, but it wasn't long before people found other uses for them.

Steroids also serve a purpose in chronic and severe asthma treatment. Although steroids do have serious side effects (so daily use isn't advised), the steroids used in asthma treatment are **corticosteroids**, not anabolic steroids. Corticosteroids are produced by the adrenal glands, not the testes; they have nothing to do with controlling muscle mass or sexual features. Nonetheless, any steroid is serious medicine. The bottom line is that steroids are never used as the **only** treatment for asthma, but in conjunction with other medication.

HOW STEROIDS WORK

Corticosteroids are used in asthma management when all else fails to control attacks. They work by stimulating the body to make more cAMP, which allows for bronchodilation and decreased mucus production. Cortisone (or glucocorticoid) controls levels of sugar, fat, and protein in the body. More important for our discussion, it controls inflammation in the body.

When the mast cells release their toxic chemicals, white blood cells rush into the area and further add to the inflammation. Cortisone (and derivatives) lower the number of inflammatory cells being drawn to the area. The fewer inflammatory cells, the sooner the inflammation goes down.

Steroids come in several forms: tablets, injections, inhaled medication, and nasal spray. The following are steroid preparations:

> prednisone
> prednisolone
> beclomethasone   dipropionate   (Vanceril   and
>   Beclovent)
> triamcinolone acetonide (Azmacort)
> flunisolide (Aerobid)
> Beconase AQ

Good Points

The best point about steroids is their effectiveness. They control the inflammation of chronic asthma. In a bronchospasm, the walls swell, narrowing the passageway. Mucus production increases, making the airway even more constricted. But steroids help to reduce the inflammation, so the airways don't remain so hypersensitive. And by decreasing mucus production, they leave the airways less irritated.

Steroids, even the corticosteroids, have severe side effects (covered below). But the inhaled preparations have far fewer side effects because the medicine is delivered directly to the airways, rather than coursing through the bloodstream.

Drawbacks

If corticosteroids are taken over a long period of time (more than two weeks), they can cause side effects. The side effects range from mild to quite serious; from slow healing of wounds to brittleness of bones to eye cataracts to adrenal gland failure.

These steroids suppress your body's natural secretion of cortisone. If taken over a long enough time, your body stops producing its own. If you're facing surgery or anything stressful, you need a boost of steroids because your body will not be putting out an extra supply to cover the emergency. There is a solution, however. People who need steroids can take them every other day instead of every day. This seems to lessen the effects on the adrenal glands. And if you take them in the morning (when your body produces most of its steroids), your adrenal glands don't seem to "notice" the added quantity.

Another drawback is that you cannot abruptly stop taking this kind of medication. Corticosteroids need to be tapered off under a doctor's supervision to allow your body to start producing its own cortisone once again. If you're taking a medicine and your doctor tells you not to stop it all at once, check with him or her whether you're using steroids, and definitely follow her instructions. Steroids are excellent at managing chronic asthma, but **you have to treat them with respect**.

Inhalant steroid sprays are best to use because the side effects are fewer. A couple of problems are hoarseness and oral thrush (a fungal infection), but these are easily managed. Just rinse your mouth after spraying or use a spacer with your inhaler.

Corticosteroids are medications reserved for the harder-to-treat asthma cases, but their side effects should not deter you from using them. For many people, they're the most effective component of the asthma medication regimen.

IMMUNOTHERAPY (ALLERGY SHOTS)

People who suffer from allergic asthma may need allergy shots in addition to asthma medicine. Immunotherapy involves a series of injections containing small amounts of the offending allergen, to lessen the patient's sensitivity to the allergen. The allergy shots encourage the body to produce more T-cells, which will suppress the IgE antibody production. (Remember how the IgE antibodies attach to the mast cells, eventually setting them off?) Allergy shots do not work for every allergy, though. They're most effective against dust, molds, cats, and pollens.

Before you and your doctor decide on immunotherapy, you should consider the feasibility of simply **avoiding** what you're allergic to. If it's cats, then either give the cat away or keep it outside. Dust, of course, is a little harder to avoid. You can't ever completely get rid of it. (In fact, you shouldn't be the housecleaner if you're allergic to dust.)

But when you have to adapt to your allergen, your doctor may consider you a good candidate for allergy shots. They are not to be undertaken lightly. If you're pregnant, or considering becoming pregnant in the near future, your doctor will not suggest immunotherapy until later. If he thinks you could benefit from the shots, he'll first want to pinpoint the specific substances that bother you. Chapter 2 discussed the types of tests doctors use to determine allergic reactions.

Administration of Shots

Doctors use two methods: the **seasonal approach**, which means giving shots for three to four months before your bad season; or the **perennial approach**, which means giving the shots year-round, building up to a maintenance level and then slowly phasing them out. The doctor prescribes the dose, but the nurse is usually the one to give the shot. And because an allergic reaction could precipitate an asthma attack, the shots are always given at the doctor's office.

You'll probably start off getting a shot (with a small dose of the offending allergen) and then waiting around the office thirty minutes to be sure you won't have a bad reaction. Reactions can occur hours later. If that happens to you, you need to call your doctor immediately. Each week you receive a larger dose of the offending allergen, as long as you're not reacting to it. The goal is the largest dose of allergen that does not precipitate a reaction. The hope is that your body will be desensitized to this particular allergen, lessening your dependency on medication.

Once you've reached that maximum dose and maintained it for a while, your doctor will reduce the shots to every two weeks. After a further period of time, and assuming you're doing well, he'll reduce them to once a month. Many people continue getting monthly allergy shots for a year or two once they're symptom-free. One friend took the shots for several years and did well enough to stop them a year ago. She tells me her asthma has worsened now that she's been off the shots, so she plans to resume taking them. The shots are no more painful than any shot, but they're sometimes inconvenient. My daughter and her friend, Megan, had to stop off at the doctor's every Thursday before soccer practice to get Megan's allergy shot. It just added to the activities of the day.

Allergic Reactions

Some people react too strongly to any dose of the offending allergen. That's the reason for hanging around the doctor's office for thirty minutes after the shot. The nurse can administer a shot of adrenaline to counteract the effect, or apply a tourniquet to slow the absorption of the substance, or both. The next time (if you're willing to continue), the doctor will lower the dose and essentially start over. Any time the shot provokes a reaction, the doctor will cut the dosage and proceed more slowly. One bad reaction doesn't mean the shots are worthless.

Bear in mind, however, that although immunotherapy may reduce your asthma symptoms, the shots alone won't **cure** your asthma. One of my son's friends gets allergy shots as part of his asthma treatment. Jeremy takes allergy shots so he can tolerate dust, pollen, and cats. They seem to work, since he spends a great deal of time at our house and we have a cat. Nonetheless, he has an inhaler to use in the event of an attack. The allergy shots clearly help him adjust to the allergens in his environment, but they have not cured his asthma. If you're one of the people who benefit from immunotherapy, the best you can hope for is a reduction in the overall asthma medication you'll need to control your attacks. But that in itself is something!

CHAPTER ◇ 10

Other Treatments

ANTIHISTAMINES

Since histamine is one of the toxic chemicals released by the mast cells, you might think an **antihistamine** would be a good medication to counter its effects. The idea sounds logical, but unfortunately, it doesn't hold up. Antihistamines are effective in controlling the symptoms of hay fever, but for some reason they don't act to dilate airways. In an asthma attack, the mast cells lining the bronchial tubes explode, constricting the airways, increasing mucus production, and causing inflammation. Antihistamines seem effective only in treating rhinitis: mast cell explosion in the nasal passages. In fact, many doctors suggest that asthmatics avoid the use of antihistamines because they can dry up the airways (as well as nasal passages) and thus make mucus plugs harder to cough up.

If your asthma is complicated with nasal disease, your doctor may recommend an antihistamine, but more likely she'll prescribe a steroid nasal spray. (Using a regular nasal spray for more than three days straight can cause severe rebound effects; you have to keep increasing the dosage of spray to keep your nose from plugging up.) The steroid sprays work differently and are meant to be used regularly. Most antihistamines have warning labels that read: Do not take this product if you have asthma . . . If you think an antihistamine might help with your nasal congestion, consult your doctor.

EXPECTORANTS

Drugstores feature shelves and shelves of medicines aimed at relieving a cough and setting one off. If you have trouble with excess mucus and can't seem to cough it up, you might think an expectorant would help. After all, the label says it will help clear your throat. Some asthmatics swear by certain brands of expectorants, but my research has shown that plain old water is just as effective. By drinking lots of fluids—preferably water—you keep yourself well hydrated, and the mucus should be easy to cough up and clear out of your throat. If you have mucus plugs blocking your airways, you probably need more help than a mere expectorant.

THE PEAK FLOW METER

The peak flow meter is a monitor of your current asthma condition. As such, it's not a medication. All it can do for you during an attack is confirm that you're having trouble expelling air.

The peak flow meter is a small, portable device that measures lung functioning. Most cost between $20 and $25. It is a tube that you hold against your mouth and seal your lips around. Always stand up when using the peak flow meter. Then simply blow out as hard and fast as you can. A needle slides up and down a scale on top of the device to register how hard you exhale. No one can totally empty his lungs of air, but try to empty as much as you can all in one breath.

The little needle should shoot up the scale. Record your score, wait a minute, and then repeat the process. When you've done it three times, use your highest score (don't average them) and compare it to your "personal best." Your doctor (who has to prescribe the meter; you can't buy it over the counter) will tell you what your personal best should be, based on your gender, height, and age. Then you can slide markers up or down on your scale to indicate the green zone (80 to 100 percent of personal best), the yellow zone (50 to 80 percent, which indicates an attack may be imminent), and the red zone (below 50 percent, which is the danger zone: call your doctor immediately!)

If you use the peak flow meter twice a day, once in the morning (when typically your airflow is worst) and again at night (or whenever you think you're having trouble), you'll readily see how well (or poorly) you're doing. Many people don't show symptoms of obstruction until they're so bad that they need emergency-room treatment. By regularly monitoring your asthma condition with the peak flow meter, you can tell earlier if your airways are heading for trouble and do something about it before it gets out of hand. Most emergency-room visits result from not having recognized early enough the warning signs of an attack.

The peak flow meter is very easy to use. Before you begin, be sure the needle is in the starting position and that nothing is clogging the scale. Using the device and recording your numbers will help assess the severity of your asthma.

Don't forget to clean your peak flow meter regularly. Just immerse the device (scale and all) in hot, soapy water, wash it, rinse it, and dry it thoroughly. (I do not recommend washing it in the dishwasher.) Keeping it clean will prevent the growth of bacteria. When you blow forcefully into the meter, mucus and germs can collect in the tube. A simple cleaning will keep the meter in good shape.

Defective Meters

Peak flow meters can be defective sometimes. If you find that the needle is very hard to move, but you're not experiencing any symptoms, see if the pharmacy will let you try another one. Michal's first peak flow meter was defective, but we were too inexperienced to know it. She kept registering in the yellow zone, and we kept waiting for the asthma attack, even though she seemed to be fine. One day I tried it myself (you really shouldn't share peak flow meters because of the risk of spreading infection), and I registered in the danger zone. Since I don't have asthma, I was naturally suspicious. We went back to the pharmacy, and the pharmacist let Michal use another meter, which she sent right up into the green zone. "Boy, it's never been this easy," she exclaimed.

"Apparently the other one was defective," the pharmacist said. "We'll send it back to the manufacturer. It doesn't happen often, but sometimes. And we never know it unless the patient brings it back."

POSTURAL DRAINAGE

Some asthmatics have trouble coughing up mucus plugs. All it takes is one mucus plug big enough to block a constricted airway, and you can stop breathing. So some people learn the technique of postural drainage to help loosen the asthmatic's mucus from his lungs. After administering a bronchodilator, the therapist (or person learning the technique) taps on the back of the asthmatic, who reclines in various positions. Varied positions are used because mucus plugs don't always block the same part of the airways. A position that dislodges the plug one time might not work the next time.

Postural drainage is not something the asthmatic can perform himself. He needs a **trained** partner who has learned the procedure from a therapist.

NEBULIZERS

Some people prefer to use a nebulizer at home instead of an MDI, which is harder to master. You can buy a nebulizer at a reasonable cost; you don't need the fanciest model. The nebulizer is a form of humidifier or vaporizer, changing liquid medicine into a mist that can be inhaled easily. The asthmatic can wear a face mask attached to the machine and read or play quietly for the ten or fifteen minutes it takes to dispense the medication. (Some dispense it in only five minutes.) If the person objects to the face mask, he can simply sit near the nebulizer so that he still breathes in the mist. People who cannot coordinate an inhaler can easily manage the nebulizer. The only drawback is that it is not as portable as the MDI. The advantage is that the mist usually penetrates deeper than the MDI.

ANXIETY AND TRANQUILIZERS

Since anxiety can sometimes precipitate an asthma attack, and heightened anxiety always makes an asthma attack worse, wouldn't it make sense to take a tranquilizer when you're feeling anxious? Some people think so, but they're **wrong**! Never take a tranquilizer if you're subject to asthma attacks or if you're in the middle of one. Tranquilizers can depress breathing and suppress coughing—the very two things you don't want to suppress during an asthma attack.

Of course, it's easier to pop a pill when stressed than to do something about the stress, but the asthmatic needs to stay away from tranquilizers. So what else can you do?

First of all, just as you do with allergens, try to avoid stress. If you always get upset when your relatives fight, try to cut down on your visits there. If your boss is unreasonable, switch jobs or file a complaint, if warranted. If you're considering medical school but can't stand chemistry or physics, consider a different profession. Of course, it's not always possible to walk away from every stressful situation. What do you do when your nerves are shot and you've having trouble keeping your asthma under control?

In cases when you can't avoid stress, you need to learn ways to adapt to it. That doesn't mean pretending it doesn't exist, or that things don't get under your skin. Rather, it means finding healthy ways to react to stressful things you can't change.

Sometimes it's merely a matter of standing up for yourself, not letting yourself be a victim. If people borrow money (or clothes or books) from you, and either don't repay you or return the stuff soiled or damaged, consider saying no to them the next time. Consider asking for restitution if the item borrowed was damaged. You'll be surprised how good you can feel about yourself just from saying no once in awhile. Oh, it takes a little getting used to. You may feel guilty at first, especially if you want everyone to like you. But ironically, most people don't truly like a pushover, and nobody respects a victim.

Sometimes all you have to do is learn to organize your time better. If you find yourself scurrying around trying to do too many things in a day, and then suffering for the next three days with asthma attacks, you're obviously not budgeting your time well. Make a list of priorities, and tackle the most important stuff first. If you run out of time in a day, you've at least done the most important stuff. Or make a list and first tackle the things you most hate to do. That way, you'll do the stuff you usually put off. Reward yourself by leaving the best things for last. Homework, for example. If you get that out of the way earlier in the day, you don't have to dread the evening, finding excuses to hide from the books.

Likewise, don't take on so many activities that you don't have any relaxing time during the day. One of Michal's friends plays soccer, volleyball, and basketball—all during the same season. She's always running from one place to another and never has time to get really good at any one of the sports. Prioritize your activities and do only those few that bring you the greatest reward or challenges. Leave yourself plenty of "down time" or "quiet time" in a day so you can unwind before hopping into bed.

STRESS REDUCTION

Learn some relaxation techniques. If you're the type who can make himself sick over giving a speech, learn how to calm down. Pregnant women use relaxation techniques to make childbirth easier; you can use the same techniques to calm yourself in stressful situations or during an asthma attack. That is not to say that relaxation techniques alone will cure your asthma attack. They don't replace medication, but they may lessen the amount of medication you need.

You can pick up any book on relaxation techniques and find something useful in it. Or listen to an audio tape on stress management. Better yet, enroll in a community class on stress reduction or ask your doctor to suggest a therapist who can show you some relaxation techniques. You don't have to commit yourself to years of therapy just to learn stress reduction techniques.

Basically, what you'll learn is how to recognize when you're becoming tense, so that you can willingly relax. That is certainly much easier said than done. First, you learn to contract your muscles, tensing them and holding the position for a number of seconds. Then you relax the muscles you've just tensed. Start with your toes and proceed through all the muscle groups up to your head. The whole process should take between twenty and thirty minutes, and you should be visibly relaxed afterward. Don't try doing this if you're pressed for time. Plan a thirty-minute block in your day, because if you're in a hurry, you won't succeed in relaxing. Sometimes it helps to listen to soothing music or the sounds of rain or ocean surf.

Some people relax by visualizing calming places and seeing themselves in them. My favorite spot to visualize has always been the ocean; specifically, a point high up on the rocks, overlooking the Atlantic at Two Lights, Maine. I actually went there to relax during exam time in college, but even in Oklahoma now, I've put myself there on many occasions. I still feel the cooling breeze, while the sun beats down on me. I can feel the salt on my face, as the tide rushes in and splashes up over the rocks. Most of all, I hear the steady pounding of the waves, and the seagulls in the distance. I rarely get to go to Two Lights anymore, but whenever I'm stressed I can put myself back there and it makes me feel good (partly because I always see myself as twenty-one).

If you're nervous about giving a speech, visualize yourself in a less threatening situation. Pretend your audience are all second-graders. Or visualize them all sitting there in their underwear. You're the only one clothed and thus in control of the situation. If you're good at visualizing things, you'll be well on your way to relaxing.

Some people meditate (and you can learn these techniques through classes or books), while others simply let their minds float, emptying their thoughts. There is no right or wrong way to relax. Whatever works to keep your heart rate down and breathing under control is right.

BIOFEEDBACK

Biofeedback is another tool the therapist uses to teach relaxation. The patient is hooked up to a machine that measures heart rate, and he's then instructed to slow it down. When the patient sees that he can actually lower the needle on the monitor simply by relaxing, he realizes that he can will himself to relax. Some therapists start out giving the patient a simple thermometer. You hold it with the mercury between your thumb and index finger, and you watch how high the mercury rises. Anxious people won't be able to raise the mercury much, for anxious people have cold hands and fingers. But as the patient focuses on raising the mercury, he's relaxing and the warmth in his fingers causes the mercury to rise. When a person can raise the mercury in the finger-held thermometer at will, he's capable of relaxing. Other biofeedback techniques follow the same principle. Some measure your heart rate, some your skin temperature, and some your muscle tension. The machine visibly displays your level of tension, and you work with the machine to relax.

The only drawback to biofeedback machines is that they're hard to translate into regular life. Once you leave the therapist's office and you can't see the dials on the machine, it's harder to remember to do what you did when you were there. Under stress, when the thermometer isn't in your hand, it's hard to get your hands to warm up and hence to relax.

The bottom line is this: Relaxing (however you do it short of alcohol or drugs) counteracts stress. The less anxious you are, the better controlled your asthma should be. For as you know, tense muscles contract and constrict. That's the last thing you need during an asthma attack.

CHAPTER 11

Emergency-Room Treatment and Hospitalization

Roger is a twelve-year-old boy who's had asthma most of his life. In fact, he's so used to his condition that when he starts coughing in the night, he knows to get up and turn on his nebulizer. One recent night was different, though.

Around 1:00 in the morning, his parents heard him coughing. His mother got up to make sure he had turned on his nebulizer. But instead of a prolonged coughing fit, Roger started to gasp for air. He clutched his throat and started turning blue.

Roger's mother called 911, while his father tried to pound his back and dislodge the suspected mucus plug. Before the rescue vehicles could arrive, Roger had already stopped breathing, and his hysterical parents thought he was dead. Nonetheless, they laid him on the floor, turned him on his side, and kept up their continuous efforts to get him to cough—and breathe.

The story has a happy ending. Roger did pull through this asthma attack and was transported to the hospital for further emergency treatment. The family learned a valuable lesson: to monitor his asthma condition throughout the day. Had Roger been using a peak flow meter, he would have known that his breathing was compromised well before his nighttime attack. Then he could have used his medication earlier to ward off the attack, probably preventing the need for emergency-room treatment.

People often end up needing the emergency room because they haven't done anything about a worsening condition. Maybe they just don't think their condition is serious enough to warrant calling a doctor. So they delay doing anything until it's too late. Those who live in the inner cities account for more emergency-room visits than their wealthier counterparts. That's not surprising, since many people can't afford regular doctor's visits or the medication needed to control their asthma. Health insurance covers most of the cost, but a sizable number of Americans do not have medical insurance. Thus, they treat the emergency room as their "regular care." They can't afford medicine otherwise, and don't seek treatment until their asthma is so severe they need a hospital.

That isn't to say that all emergency-room visits are the result of inadequate medical attention. Despite all your efforts to follow your medication regimen, you may still end up needing extra help. At the first sign your regular medication isn't working (for example, if you don't get any relief after using your regular inhaler twice), call your doctor. Or if you have more breathing trouble than usual while not exerting yourself as much, call your doctor. You aren't bothering your doctor. He prefers you to call when things seem different, since it saves him from possible complications. Besides, you're paying for this care.

Asthmatics more often need emergency-room treatment during the hours of 7 am and noon, which probably reflects the fact that asthma is worse in the morning and should improve as the day wears on. If your asthma symptoms don't improve throughout the day, that's another reason to call your doctor.

If you're subject to food allergies or allergic to bee stings, you should always have adrenaline on hand. Doctors can prescribe you an Epi Pen, which contains a measured dose of adrenaline. All you have to do is press the Epi Pen against your thigh (when suffering an allergic reaction), and it'll release the adrenaline. With anaphylaxis, your body shuts down. You need help immediately. You won't usually have time to run to your doctor's.

THE EMERGENCY ROOM

If you need to go to the emergency room because you're having trouble breathing and your regular medicine isn't helping, call ahead to the E.R. and let them know you're coming. Make sure you know what medicine you've been taking. That means dosage as well as the time you took it.

When you arrive in the emergency room, a medical person (often a nurse) will have you fill out information regarding the problem, as well as verifying your insurance coverage. Make sure you're carrying your health insurance card. Emergency rooms don't treat their patients on a first-come, first-served basis. They treat the life-threatening cases first and then all others. If you're not in acute distress, they may ask you to take a seat in the waiting area until they can accommodate you in a treatment room. If you are having a lot of trouble breathing, make sure you convey that to the first person you talk to. An asthmatic in acute distress constitutes a priority case, and you'll be given a room immediately.

If you've never seen the inside of an emergency room, you may be disturbed by the chaos, the noise and bustling about. Most E.R.s don't even have individual treatment rooms. The nurses simply pull curtains around your bed to give you some privacy, but you can hear what's going on in the bed beside you, and vice versa. While you're waiting for your doctor, practice some relaxation techniques. Calm yourself down so their treatments will have a better chance of working.

Ask the nurse to call your regular physician, if you haven't already done so. They are supposed to do that if you request it, and you'll probably get better treatment if you have a doctor they can converse with. Don't expect coddling or nurturing from emergency room doctors and nurses. These professionals are always reacting to a crisis. They haven't the time or energy to establish a "relationship." As long as they know their job, that's what matters. Sometimes you'll be lucky and get a nurturing, attentive nurse or doctor. If you get one of these nurturing types, be sure you later send him or her a thank-you note. Professionals like to be thanked as much as the next person. And who knows? You might need help again.

More than likely, the first thing the doctor will order is an adrenaline injection. If the first shot fails to help your breathing, she'll order a second, followed by a beta-2-stimulating bronchodilator given via a nebulizer. (Remember, the nebulizer's mist can penetrate deeper than the inhaler.)

You'll probably be given a chest x-ray to rule out

pneumonia or air in your chest, and given oxygen if you seem to need it.

Theophylline may be given intravenously for a while to stabilize you, so it's vital for you to know your theophylline medication regimen. And not simply what your doctor prescribed, but what you've actually taken! In order to avoid giving you a toxic dose, they'll probably run a blood level on you.

Some people have to go to the emergency room two or three times in a day. Doctors will not resent you if you're complying with the medication regimen but just having unusual difficulty. It's relieving to know that there are always people to treat you when your regular medicine isn't working. The adrenaline, intravenous theophylline, and nebulizing beta-2-stimulating medication will continue until you're either safe to discharge or hospitalized. If you're discharged, you'll be given instructions and prescriptions (or medicine) and no doubt urged to call your regular physician for follow-up. Then you should go home and relax as much as possible.

STATUS ASTHMATICUS

Status asthmaticus is the scariest condition you can have. It means your condition is life-threatening, and you will be hospitalized. You'll have serious narrowing of your airways, heavy mucus secretion, and mucus plugging of your bronchial tubes.

Do not panic! Even if the adrenaline injections or intravenous theophylline fail to improve your asthma, there are other options. You aren't necessarily going to die.

First, the nurses may try bronchial suctioning in an effort to remove as much mucus as possible from your airways. It's not a painful procedure, but it's uncomfortable.

If they suspect you're not getting enough oxygen, or getting rid of enough carbon dioxide, doctors will order arterial blood gases. This procedure is painful because the technician needs to stick a needle in an artery, not a vein, to draw out blood. Blood gases are the most important test to measure the oxygen and carbon dioxide in your blood. If the test reveals excessively low oxygen and excessively high carbon dioxide, you'll be put on a respirator.

The respirator tube is inserted through your nose or mouth down into your windpipe. Then it's attached to a machine at your bedside that will inflate your lungs at a certain rate and depth. In other words, the respirator takes over the job of breathing for you and oxygenating your blood. You'll probably remain on the respirator for twelve to forty-eight hours so it can do the job of increasing the oxygen in your blood and decreasing the carbon dioxide. Doctors don't want you to stay on a respirator any longer than necessary; it's important to resume breathing on your own as soon as possible.

Will the respirator hurt you? Not necessarily, but it depends on the nurse's technique. He could injure your windpipe inserting or removing the respirator tube, but the damage would be minimal. There's some risk of infection, but all things considered, the respirator is a lifesaving invention.

With all this concentrated attention and bedrest, you should recover within a few days and be released from the hospital. If you've had a relapse requiring emergency-room care or hospitalization, you're at greater risk for another relapse. You need to take things as easy as possible, follow your medication regimen to the letter, and watch for early signs of trouble.

Believe it or not, some people actually look forward to these brief hospitalizations, if only for the rest and special attention. It's comforting to know that help is always available.

PART ◇ IV

LIVING WITH ASTHMA

CHAPTER 12

Leading a Normal Life

C herlene recently moved to Tulsa from California. Being a new girl in school, she didn't want to attract a lot of attention to herself. Not the negative kind, anyway. She'd grown up with kids in her old school, and they all knew she had asthma. The teachers all knew about her condition, too, and when she felt her breathing was getting bad, she'd tell the teacher she needed to go use her inhaler. It was no big deal.

But Tulsa was a bigger place than where she used to live, and while she did tell some teachers she had asthma, she didn't tell them all. Nor did she devise a plan in case she had an attack during class. She hadn't had many attacks in the past, so she figured she'd just see how things went the first few weeks.

Tulsa is known for its high pollen and mold counts, so it didn't take long before Cherlene started to react. In history class one day, she started getting a headache. She knew headaches often preceded her asthma attacks, but she prayed this time she could hang on. Her inhaler was in her purse, but she didn't want to pull it out in the middle of class.

She tried to concentrate on the teacher's lecture. But she could feel her chest tightening, and she stretched her diaphragm a little to make it easier to breathe. She checked the clock; twenty more minutes left in class. She should really use her inhaler, she knew, but class was almost over. Surely she could hang on just for a few more minutes.

A few minutes went by. Cherlene stifled a cough. Her chest was heaving, and the more she fought off the asthma attack, the worse it got. She wanted to run out of the classroom. She glanced around to see if anyone was noticing. She looked at the clock. Why wasn't it moving faster? And then she started to cough. And wheeze, and clutch at her throat. She reached in her purse for her inhaler; she had to breathe. The teacher stopped talking. Everyone turned in their seats to look at the new kid, gasping and coughing and fumbling through her purse. As she pulled out her inhaler, all eyes were on her, and she realized that ignoring the attack had made it all the worse. She could have been in the bathroom or the nurse's station by now, or even in the hallway, inhaling the spray. But because she waited so long, now she had to use it in front of everyone . . .

ADVISING YOUR TEACHERS

When you have asthma and go to school, you face one of two things. Either you're going to miss an awful lot of school, or you're going to have to use your medicine at school once in a while. In either case, you need to let your teachers, the school nurse, the principal, and the guidance counselor know about your condition.

Asthma is nothing to be ashamed of, but if people witness an attack, it may look scary to them. And you may feel as if you're making a spectacle of yourself. The minute you discover you have asthma, arrange a meeting with your teachers and counselor. Maybe your doctor can write a letter explaining your asthma triggers and a plan of action—for example, what medicine you should take in the event of an attack. Then you and your parents should decide:

1. Whether you should carry your medicine yourself and administer it when **you** feel the need.
2. At what point the teachers should call your parents when you're having trouble.
3. Under what circumstances the school should call an ambulance.

The school will probably never have to call that ambulance, but at least you and they will know when they should. If you and your parents believe your teachers are capable of handling any emergency, you'll feel safer and probably miss less school.

If you have any food allergies, make sure **everyone** knows about it, so that you're never urged to eat something you shouldn't. At your age your peers may egg you on. Everyone needs to know the consequences of your eating the forbidden food, and you should carry an Epi Pen just in case something slips by you.

When you talk with school personnel, be sure to include your gym teacher as well. He or she especially needs to know any limitations you have, for example, staying indoors on cold and windy days. If you can't handle certain activities, try to suggest alternatives so you don't have to flunk class. One student told me she barely made it out of high school because she kept flunking gym class. And she flunked because she missed so many classes.

AT WORK

If you have a job (part-time or otherwise), you owe it to your employer to explain your asthma and asthma triggers. He or she needs to know in case you're absent a lot. He also needs to know what to do in the event of an asthma attack. You may be reluctant to bring the subject up in an interview if you think it might dissuade him or her from hiring you. If he doesn't ask about medical problems, you don't necessarily have to bring it up prior to getting hired. But once you are working for him, you owe it to him, as well as yourself, to be honest about your health and how you plan to respond to an asthma attack.

Take stock of your work environment, too, because it's not uncommon for certain chemicals or fumes at work to provoke an asthma attack. If you do find yourself having more breathing trouble at work than at home, decide what you're allergic to and if you can avoid the allergen. If you can't, you may have to find a different job.

CARRYING YOUR OWN MEDICINE

Parents may not want younger children to carry inhalers to school, but those old enough to know when and how to use them should be allowed to do so at their discretion. Of course, not all schools agree with my philosophy. Check out where **your** school stands on the issue. Some schools prefer for you to go to the nurse's office to take your medicine. It's probably a good idea for the school nurse to know you're having trouble, but sometimes you won't have time to ask permission and then walk over there. Some teachers may prefer you to step outside to the hall and use your inhaler, or ask permission to go to the bathroom. Whatever decision is made, it should be agreeable to both of you. If you don't feel comfortable leaving your inhaler in the nurse's office, ask your doctor to talk with the nurse about giving you that responsibility. As long as you're responsible, you should carry your own medicine. At the first sign the medicine isn't working, notify your teacher and then the school nurse. Don't delay treatment because you don't want to draw attention to yourself. Chances are, like Cherlene, you'll end up drawing more attention by initially doing nothing.

If your school refuses to let you carry your own medicine despite your doctor's intervention, keep making an issue out of it. Just last year a student died in school because her teacher wouldn't give her permission to use her inhaler. The teacher had no idea the girl would die of an asthma attack, but within minutes, that's exactly what happened. Sometimes a person just doesn't have time to run and find the school nurse.

KEEPING ASTHMA A SECRET

When you're a teenager, the last thing you want is to be different from everyone else. And asthma does make you different. It's best not to try to keep the condition a secret, as if you're ashamed of having it. After all, there is no cure for asthma, only medication to manage it. And it's not your fault that you've got asthma. People are born with the tendency to develop asthma, or they're not.

Letting your friends know about your asthma makes it easier to go ahead and use your inhaler when you first feel the need. If everyone knows you sometimes have trouble breathing and need to use an inhaler, they won't be especially surprised when they see you using one. If they know what your asthma is like, they won't necessarily overreact when they see you wheezing. And if they remain calm, it helps you to remain calm.

Another girl on Michal's soccer team had asthma. At one point during a game, Katherine hollered over to me, "Tell my mom I need my inhaler."

No one seemed particularly frightened or even concerned about her using an inhaler. Since everyone on Michal's team knows that she is supposed to use her inhaler before practices and games, her teammates sometimes remind her. No one seems to act as if it's a handicap, probably because Michal and her teammate, Katherine, don't consider it one.

Some people actually deny to themselves (as well as their friends) that they've got asthma or that anything's wrong. Even if you pretend you don't have asthma and don't need medication, it won't make the condition go away. If anything, you'll probably end up either in the emergency room or at the hospital because you've failed to deal with the problem.

Telling your friends about asthma shouldn't be a big deal. If they see your inhaler, you can explain why you carry it. Whenever Michal sees a person carrying an MDI around, she asks, "Oh, do you have asthma?" (It hasn't occurred to her that some people might not want to talk about it.) For Michal, it was a relief to have asthma diagnosed. That explained her trouble breathing whenever she ran too much in soccer games. "At least now people know there's something officially wrong. I'm not just out of shape," she has said.

Bringing the subject out in the open will encourage

others to speak more openly. Whenever I mention I'm writing a book on asthma, someone within voice range hears and says, "Oh, I have asthma, too." Or else her Aunt Sue Ellen has it, or Cousin Freddy had it as a baby. You'll be surprised how common asthma is.

Offer to give a speech on asthma. Well, I don't know anyone who willingly wants to give a speech, but if you have to talk on some subject for five minutes for class, you might as well make it something you know well. Most people would be interested to hear your asthma experience. Call it curiosity or nosiness, but I guarantee you'll have plenty to talk about for five minutes.

If you're the organizing type, start an asthma support group. Plenty of resources are available; see the Appendix for an idea of where to start. Finding yourself in the company of so many others with asthma should give you a better sense of your possibilities, rather than limitations.

PLAYING SPORTS

The asthmatic can still play sports. As I mentioned earlier, some sports are more realistic than others. And you'll probably have to premedicate, but don't forgo a little exercise because you fear an asthma attack.

My son takes tae kwon do lessons in town. His instructor, Jim Hammons, is a national tae kwon do black belt champion and has so many trophies that they fill one corner of the workout room. If you saw Mr. Hammons you wouldn't be surprised; he can effortlessly put his foot through four boards from a standing position. When he spars, he tackles six or seven kids at once and still manages to stay on his feet.

One day while I was waiting for my son to finish class, Mr. Hammons walked by and peered over my shoulder.

When he saw I was reading a book on asthma, he said, "Oh, I have asthma. In fact, that's why I first learned tae kwon do. I couldn't play basketball; in fact, I couldn't do much of anything like that. I couldn't even make it through my tae kwon do classes at first without resting. That was fifteen years ago."

Tae kwon do is a form of martial arts. Because it strengthens the upper body and lungs, it is excellent for improving overall lung functioning in asthmatics. Mr. Hammons rarely needs his asthma medicine now, and the only time his asthma symptoms have flared up was when he stopped working out while recovering from a neck injury.

The moral of this story is that exercise is **good** for the asthmatic. As your overall fitness improves, you'll be able to play longer and harder. And as a result, your self-esteem will grow.

That doesn't mean you can tackle any sport. Some are better than others. Talk with your doctor about sports you want to play. Sports that don't require a lot of running are the best ones for you: baseball, tennis, swimming, golf, and bicycling. Learn to recognize weather conditions that trigger your asthma. When it's humid and windless, air pollution builds up more quickly. Practice indoors on days like that, or take more frequent breaks. If you like skiing, wear a ski mask or scarf over your mouth. Breathing your own moist air will be better on your airways than a fresh gulp of frosty cold air.

One of my friends spent a rather boring childhood—or at least a sedentary one. She couldn't play any sports because her asthma was so bad. Believe it or not, one day she decided she was tired of always sitting out activities. Little by little she involved herself in aerobic sports, and by now she teaches an aerobics fitness class here in town.

Most of us were surprised to learn she had asthma because she was so athletic. She attributes her well-being to working out, starting slowly and building up her endurance and lung capacity. Aerobic activities are of course the hardest on your heart and lungs, but the best for them in the long run. Kristina is proof that your will can be a great asset in getting well.

Make sure you know when you **shouldn't** work out. Those will be the times when your peak flow meter shows that your breathing is compromised even if you aren't having an actual attack. Most asthmatics can recognize signs of an imminent attack. Some get headaches first, feel "spacey, moody, restless, or feverish." Some complain of a scratchy throat or that they feel weak. Be sure you can tell the difference between normal side effects of your medication and symptoms of a coming asthma attack. Michal's legs get weak right after she's used her inhaler. It doesn't signify an asthma attack; it's just a side effect she's learned to adapt to.

If you find yourself feeling unlike yourself, don't work out. Keep your medication handy, and pass on the activity for the moment.

DANCING

People who don't have asthma can't imagine all the ways the condition can interfere with your social life. If you can't exercise very much, how are you going to dance? Dancing, after all, is an aerobic activity. Then, too, consider the environment of some dance places. They're smoky, as a rule. Put the smoky environment together with the energy needed for dancing, and you've got the perfect conditions for an asthma attack. So what do you do?

Well, you have three choices. You can tell people you hate dancing and avoid the activity in the first place (which will decrease your opportunities to meet people). You can dance in the smoky environment and see how long you can last without an attack. Or you can work out aerobically so that you're in better shape to dance. Then, dance only in the right conditions. Stay away from smoky places and sit down when you're feeling stressed. Make sure your partner knows you have asthma, and if you're allergic to strong colognes, tell him, so his after-shave doesn't set off your coughing. Dancing is indeed hard for some asthmatics, but you can still participate by recognizing and respecting your limitations.

SINGING

Singing may be hard, too, but it helps build up your lungs, and it's definitely worth doing. Don't assume that you can't be in chorus or the church choir. Singing helps with breathing, and while it's hard to do as an asthmatic, it'll improve your breathing control.

By now you should see that asthma doesn't have to be a crippling disease. Sure, it may limit you somewhat, but all you need to do is learn to work within those limitations. One young girl I know has cystic fibrosis (a condition that sometimes resembles asthma). Sandy is a great little actress, but when she first tried out for plays, she never got the parts. Finally, a teacher confessed to her mother that she was afraid to give Sandy a major role in case she got "sick" and ended up missing school.

Sandy's mother was incensed. "Treat her like anyone else," she said. "Surely you have understudies."

And so the teacher offered Sandy a part, and though Sandy got sick and missed some rehearsals, she didn't miss the play. Her spirits soared too once she was given the opportunity to "be like everyone else."

Hard as it is, sometimes YOU have to demand that others stop coddling you. You can do much more than you possibly think. And no doubt more than others think you can do. Stretch those horizons . . . Raise those expectations . . .

CHAPTER 13

Managing Your Asthma "Triggers"

A Rainbow vacuum cleaner salesman came to our house to demonstrate the benefits of his water-filled vacuum cleaner. He claimed, and certainly seemed to prove, that his vacuum cleaner sucked up more dust and dirt than a conventional vacuum cleaner such as ours. "It also improves air quality for the asthmatic," he said.

My thoughts immediately turned to Michal. "Hey, you ought to come out and see this," I called to her.

The salesman looked around our recently vacuumed living room. "Now, I'm not saying you're a lousy house-keeper," he told me. "But I'm going to show you what your regular vacuum cleaner missed."

He put a filter on his vacuum cleaner and then started to clean. Within a minute or two, he stopped and removed the filter. It was filthy.

Michal, my husband, and I watched with disgust. We'd been breathing that air?

"That's what your cleaner missed," he said. "Now, let's

shake some of this back into the air and try again, using this other attachment."

Later, he offered to clean the pillows on the divan. He showed how much dust had been buried in the pillows without our even suspecting such.

Before he finished, Michal started to have trouble breathing and eventually needed her inhaler. It wasn't the vacuum cleaner's fault; it was all the dust and dirt the salesman has stirred up to demonstrate his product for us. It proved his point, but it caused an asthma attack in the process. That was our first inkling that Michal's asthma was set off by more than just hard exercising . . .

AVOIDANCE IS BEST

If you're an asthmatic and want to avoid attacks, the best thing you can do is to avoid the allergens that set you off. If strong odors set you off, avoid them. If your folks are painting the house, spend the first forty-eight hours with a friend, so you don't inhale the fumes. If you're designated the oven-cleaner, delegate the task to a sibling (with your parent's approval). Asthmatics should not be exposed to sprays and other chemicals that could set off their asthma. Likewise, you can't be the tub-scrubber or tile cleaner. You shouldn't use any aerosol products except your inhaler. That means, no spray perfumes or hair spray.

If you're allergic to perfumes, make sure your friends know this as well. **You** may know not to wear the stuff yourself, but you probably can't tolerate being around **others** who are wearing heavy colognes. And that goes for boyfriends, too. If their after-shave is overpowering, you're not going to be able to tolerate their company for long.

Animals

What if you're allergic to cats and dogs? Your doctor will probably tell you to get rid of any house pets. If you and your family can stand it, find your pets a nice home. Don't claim you've banished the pet, if you really haven't. Your asthma symptoms will show, and the doctor will be misled as to their causes.

We have both dogs and a cat at our house, and it would be heartbreaking if we were told to get rid of them because of Michal's asthma. (Fortunately, she doesn't appear to be allergic to animal dander.) If your pet is too much a part of the family, then at least keep all pets out of the asthmatic's bedroom. Better yet, keep the pet outdoors.

Pets are good stress reducers. If you can't tolerate the fluffy, furry kind, then consider getting tropical fish. Fish are relaxing to watch and fairly easy to care for. And they're the perfect "pets" for people with asthma.

Food Allergies

If you have food allergies, stay away from the offending substances. Before you buy anything, check the ingredients. If you're at a party, check with the hostess to make sure all ingredients are safe. And if you're not sure, don't eat it! Keep an Epi Pen with you in case of a reaction. Food allergies, while rare, are very serious.

Dust, Pollen, Mold

If we could avoid dust, even we nonasthmatics would avoid it. Obviously, however, you can't totally eliminate or avoid dust. But there are some things you can do to keep it at a minimum. Here's the good news: You, the asthmatic, should never do the dusting or vacuuming. In fact, if you have a low tolerance to dust (and some people react worse than others), you will want to be somewhere else when the house is being cleaned.

Carpets are notorious for hanging onto dust. A vacuum cleaner may get most of the surface dust, but it doesn't get the mites that cling to the carpet fibers. Better to replace any carpeting (at least in your bedroom) with wood flooring and surface rugs that can be washed regularly. Keep areas around your bed especially clean. That means washing the baseboards around the walls nearest the bed. Using wet rags is better than a feather duster. The moisture will absorb more of the dust. Wash bedding (pillows, sheets, quilts, mattress pads) often. And use foam pillows that can also be washed. Enclose the mattress in plastic; then you don't have to worry about mites working their way into mattresses.

If you spot any cockroaches in your house, have someone spray to get rid of them. Cockroach parts can be a big component of dust. No one really likes to think she shares her house with cockroaches, but their presence doesn't mean you live in substandard housing. Cockroaches are everywhere that food is; they like to hide during the day and come out at night. If you live in a duplex or apartment, your neighbors are going to have to fumigate as well because the bugs can hide in **their** place while **your place** is getting the scrub-down. Give the cockroaches time and they'll be back.

If pollen bothers you, there are certain things you can do to minimize your exposure. During pollination season, stay inside as much as possible. Use the air conditioner, and close all windows. That fresh air outside is going to be filled with pollen. If you have to work outside in the yard, wear a dust mask. You may look funny, but it'll help keep the pollen out of your nose. More good news: If you suffer from grass allergies, you shouldn't be the lawnmower in the family.

Pay attention to broadcast pollen counts. In areas where pollen and molds are high (such as Tulsa), television channels announce the counts daily. You can therefore plan ahead to stay inside on especially high-count days.

Check with your doctor to see if you'd be helped by allergy shots.

If you're allergic to molds, you may have to forgo having plants in your house. If you can't do without at least a few houseplants, just don't keep them in your bedroom where you spend most of your time. Make sure your shower stalls and curtains are cleaned regularly (and not by you). You can throw most shower curtains right in the washer and then hang them up to dry. Any place in the house that attracts moisture is a breeding ground for mold.

If you have a dehumidifier, which is a good thing to take the moisture out of the air, make sure it's emptied and cleaned regularly to avoid bacteria building up in the dehumidifier itself. The same thing goes for vaporizers. Vaporizers are wonderful inventions for adding moisture and menthol to the air, but they're also capable of growing mold if they're not cleaned daily.

EXERCISE

You can still exercise—and should—to keep your heart and lungs in good shape. But if exercising provokes an asthma attack, you need to take some precautions. Be sure to premedicate and leave enough time for the medication to kick in before attempting to play. The directions on most bronchodilators suggest that you use them fifteen minutes before exercising. They'll be effective for three to four hours. Obviously, then, you don't want to use them and then run onto the field. The medication won't have had time to work, and within six to eight minutes of exercising you'll probably have an asthma attack. Likewise, keep your inhaler with you. If your activity runs longer than four hours, you'll probably need another dose.

Be sensitive to the weather conditions that best provoke your attacks. If it's cold weather, don't be the one to shovel snow out of your driveway. If you have to be out, wear a face mask or scarf, so that you're not breathing in that frosty, cold air. If running against the wind provokes an attack, then try to run with the wind at your back. Keep a scarf handy for the return **walk** home.

Before any exercise, be sure to warm up well, and cool down afterward. Do a lot of stretching and breathing exercises. The better prepared you are to exercise, the fewer the complications.

SMOKE

Most asthmatics have trouble breathing in smoky environments. Wood stoves and fireplaces are bad on an asthmatic, but coal-burning stoves are even worse. If you have asthma and are bothered by the smoke, talk to your doctor about your options. He or she might be in a better position to convince your parents that they should switch to another form of heating. Indeed, fireplaces are romantic settings, but if you get an asthma attack because of the smoke, you're not going to be in a romantic mood for long . . .

Likewise, you need to stay out of places where people are smoking. You have the right to ask people not to smoke in your own home. Of course, if it's your parents' friends who are doing the smoking, you may need to enlist your doctor's support in confronting your parents. I was surprised at the number of asthmatics who have at least one smoking parent. If concern for their own health doesn't motivate your parents to quit smoking, perhaps concern for **your** health might. Secondhand smoke (which comes from others' smoking) is reportedly as detrimental as your own smoking. If you can't control your smoking environment, and it's hard to do that in other people's houses, take yourself out of that environment. Why risk an asthma attack?

THE DANGERS OF SMOKING

You've all heard the lectures on smoking and your health. If you haven't heard it from school, you should have heard it from your doctor. The asthmatic's lungs have a hard enough job getting an adequate air supply. Why make it even harder by smoking?

Cigarettes contain a number of irritants that can cause bronchospasms. Not only that, but smoking damages the cilia—the hairlike structures that line your nasal passages and airways. The cilia keep the mucus moving and from clogging your airways. You damage them; you're facing more immovable mucus plugs.

Smoking also interferes with your theophylline level. Your body processes the theophylline faster; hence, you need a larger dose of the medicine than the nonsmoker.

But most dangerous of all: Smoking can cause emphysema. Have you ever seen a person with emphysema? It's a permanently disabling disease. Once the air sacs in your lungs are destroyed, you've lost your ability to exchange oxygen and carbon dioxide. I have an uncle with emphysema. He's probably smoked for fifty or sixty years, even though he knew it was ruining his health. Because of his emphysema, he also has congestive heart failure. It's hard on your heart when your lungs can't add much oxygen to your blood. He lives in a two-story house but is now confined to the first floor. His family had to create a bedroom out of the parlor and a bathroom out of a small office. Uncle Henry is tired most of the time. He can't climb the stairs anymore; he has oxygen on hand because his breathing is so labored, and he's in and out of the hospital. He has to take naps three or four times a day, and he certainly can't drive a car anymore.

Uncle Henry is seventy-four, four years older than my father. Dad, who never smoked, continues to work and recently climbed the Precipice Trail on the east face of Champlain Mountain in Bar Harbor, Maine. An ascent of 1,058 feet. Uncle Henry will never climb any mountains . . .

When I questioned my students and friends, I was surprised to learn how many still smoked despite their asthma. Some, I suspect, smoke to deny the seriousness of their condition. They light up, puff a little, choke, gasp for air, and then take another drag on the cigarette. Smoking is supposedly cool. It's grownup. It's a status thing. But the truth is: Smoking is an addiction, and it's very hard to stop. People, like my uncle, keep smoking because it's too much of an effort to stop. The smoker probably uses more medication, needs the emergency room more often, and is hospitalized more often than the nonsmoking asthmatic.

If you're a smoker, consider quitting. Join a program that helps people stop smoking. It's not always something you can do "cold turkey." Get your buddies to quit along with you; it's harder to stop smoking when all your friends still do it around you. Be honest with your doctors if you continue to smoke. Pretending you aren't smoking when you are deceives no one. People can smell it on your clothes and in your hair. Your fingers turn a mustard shade of yellow, and your breath has a stale smell even if you try to cover it up with mints. If you're getting theophylline, you especially need to remind the doctor you smoke; you'll need a larger dose. Even if you don't use theophylline, you're stressing your airways by smoking and will no doubt need more of whatever medication you're using to control your asthma symptoms.

Whatever your asthma triggers, you can usually manage by either avoiding them or medicating against them (including allergy shots), and by using stress reduction techniques. Take control, rather than let your environment control you. It's not as hard as you think . . .

CHAPTER 14

Getting Along with
Your Family

A s I mentioned at the outset of this book, asthma affects families, not just individuals. I can think of no better example than Charlie's case.

Charlie isn't the one with asthma. His younger brother has it. Charlie was four when his brother, Jordan, was diagnosed with asthma at eighteen months. Suddenly, Charlie's whole world changed. Both parents became obsessed over Jordan at night, worrying every time he coughed, surrounding him with nebulizers and vaporizers and humidifiers. Whenever Jordan got a cold, their mother called the doctor immediately. Whenever Charlie got a cold, their mother said, "Well, you're the strong one. It won't last." To get Jordan to take his medicine, their mother offered him little rewards. Charlie didn't have to take any medicine, so he never got any rewards. Jordan grew up pampered; Charlie grew up bitter.

As teenagers, the situation reversed. Charlie got to play sports, but Jordan didn't. His parents thought his asthma

was too severe. Jordan hated going to his brother's baseball games, just sitting there watching everyone else
having a good time. He resented not getting to play
outside in cold, snowy weather.

"I hated myself for being different," Jordan told me.
"Charlie always got to do the fun things. Mom wouldn't
let me out of her sight. She even called my teachers to
make sure I stayed in on windy days.

"I hated Charlie, too. He was healthy; I wasn't. I know
it wasn't his fault, but I still thought it wasn't fair. Why
did I have to get this asthma? Why couldn't he have it,
too?"

Charlie adds, "I'm not bitter anymore. I used to think
my folks liked Jordan better. After all, they were always
focused on him. It's kind of weird, but there were times I
actually wished I had asthma instead of Jordan. Then I'd
get all that attention."

It wasn't until college that the brothers began to ap-
preciate each other. Charlie encouraged Jordan to join the
swim team and went to his meets. Jordan shared with
Charlie his frustration about feeling "like an invalid." And
one day, their mother admitted to them that she'd always
felt guilty for "giving Jordan asthma." Her father and
grandmother had had asthma, and back then, it was harder
to treat. When their mother realized that Jordan had his
asthma under control and really wasn't an invalid, she
stopped wallowing in guilt. But giving up her overprotec-
tiveness was a long process . . .

YOUR FEELINGS

If you're the only one with asthma in your family, you
may feel more isolated. Many families have more than
one member with asthma, and so they become allies. In

any event, you're bound to have a myriad of conflicting feelings: overprotected on the one hand, and denied the right to live a normal life on the other. You may resent your parents' focusing so much attention on you, or you may be embarrassed that your asthma causes the family vacation plans to change.

Some asthmatics simply **deny** that they have any serious illness. They pretend they're not that sick and often don't comply with their medication regimen. As a result, they probably end up in the emergency room more often and have greater complications than more compliant asthmatics. They also take more risks. Deniers probably smoke; they refuse to believe they're really allergic to anything, so they continue to test their environment. Deniers are probably angry people who don't want to view themselves as being "handicapped." They, no doubt, frighten a lot of people around them who care about their health.

Some asthmatics tell me they feel **guilty**. Because their parents are so attentive, they think they've turned their family upside down. Vacations are planned around the asthmatic's needs; medical bills mount, and babysitters are few. While it probably isn't true, many think their siblings resent them. Many think their doctors are fed up with yet one more midnight call. It's not surprising if you feel guilty some of the time. As Americans, we've been encouraged to feel guilty over lots of things. It's supposed to keep us humble, but usually all guilt does is immobilize us. As long as we punish ourselves with guilt, things don't have to change.

If you strip away some of the other emotions, you're bound to come down to **anger**. Anger at a lot of things. One man I know told me that when he was a kid he was angry all the time. He'd sit in the window and watch other kids playing, doing all the things he wasn't allowed to do. He was angry at these kids for being healthy; he was angry at himself for **not** being healthy, and he was angry at the doctors who couldn't **make** him healthy. Being angry doesn't make you a bad person. It's a logical response to a difficult situation. But anger isn't particularly useful unless it mobilizes you to change your situation. You're right: It isn't fair that you have asthma and have such trouble breathing. So what are you going to do about it? Being angry and doing nothing contributes to depression.

It's okay to resent your healthier siblings or parents. You might be surprised to know, though, that they probably envy **you** at times. For every disadvantage, they see an advantage. Some might even want to trade places with you—temporarily, at least.

Until the novelty wears off, or you have a severe attack, you may actually **enjoy** your status as an asthmatic. You will get a lot of attention from your doctor, teachers, parents, and coaches. Until they start curtailing your activities, you'll probably have nothing to gripe about. After all, who among us gets too much attention?

Some asthmatics are **worried** about having an asthma attack in public. Once Michal had an attack during a soccer game. She took a time out to use her inhaler, and no one seemed to notice. Nonetheless, Michal said to me afterward, "Did you see me trying to catch my breath? I was really making a spectacle out of myself."

"I didn't even notice you were having trouble," I said, feeling a little guilty because I hadn't noticed.

"Well, everyone else noticed. Sharon probably thought I was faking. I didn't have asthma attacks last year when I played on her team. She kept looking at me funny. I know she thought I looked stupid."

The reality was that Sharon had probably been more interested in getting the ball away from Michal than in whatever was going on with Michal's breathing. I don't think she gave it a second thought. It's just that when you're in a situation you can't always control, you often think everyone in the world is watching. And you naturally get embarrassed.

Another friend told me he was always afraid he was going to have an asthma attack in school. The more he worried about it, the greater the likelihood that he would have an attack. A shy young man, he already thought he stuck out, and so he didn't want to draw any more attention to himself than necessary.

Finally, particularly if you have asthma that's difficult to control, you may be **scared of dying**. While it's true that people do die from asthma complications—even in the hospital— it's usually because they've delayed attending to their symptoms. And even so, it's a rare event. But it's easy to understand why anyone who's ever suffered that choking feeling would be anxious.

I have not had an asthma attack, but back in high school, I had a condition that made it difficult for me to swallow. Whenever I tried to swallow, I couldn't. My muscles just didn't want to work. It was some form of anxiety attack. Anyway, the harder I tried to swallow, the more frantic I'd become because I couldn't. Somehow not being able to swallow—even liquids—made me think I was going to die. I didn't dare eat in the cafeteria anymore because I might end up choking on the food in front of 1,100 kids. One night (before I got medicine to fix this odd condition), I put all my favorite records on the stereo. I hauled out all my favorite possessions and then sat in the living room, certain I was going to die then and there. It was an out-of-control, awful feeling.

When you sometimes can't breathe, I imagine the experience to be similar to when I couldn't swallow. Only scarier, because you can only last minutes without air. Just remember that panic makes asthma much worse. If you know that those around you know how to respond in an emergency, you may feel less anxious. Never travel without your inhaler, or an Epi Pen if you have allergies. Sometimes, just knowing relief is at hand will keep you calm. Whenever Michal visits friends overnight, particularly friends whose parents smoke, she takes her inhaler. Asthma attacks are scary events, but if you plan for any emergency, you should feel less out of control.

SOLUTIONS

1. **Try to lead as normal a life as possible.** Find out your asthma triggers and do something about them. That might mean avoiding them, medicating against them, or minimizing them. Follow your doctor's instructions and medication regimen. Take your medications as prescribed, too, not just when you're feeling bad. Some medicines work only by building up in your bloodstream, so you can't just take them when you feel like it. If you work *with* your doctor instead of *against* her, you're more likely to have fewer complications. And you'll feel less guilty calling your doctor in the middle of the night. If you don't agree with something, talk it over with your doctor. Pretending to go along with her wishes when you aren't only confuses her about your continuing symptoms. Know all your warning signs of trouble and don't delay treatment.

2. **Don't hide your feelings; bring them out in the open.** That doesn't mean sharing every hurtful thought you've ever had toward someone. It means recognizing your

anger, your envy, and your fears and then doing something positive with those strong emotions. Talk to your doctor about your limitations; maybe you don't have as many limitations as you think. If you're having trouble with overprotective parents (or siblings), get them all together and tell them how you feel. Concentrate on how you feel, not on attacking their behavior. People who tend to be overprotective often feel guilty, conflicted, or fearful of losing you. Sometimes, they're scared because they love something (you) so much and just can't bear the thought of losing it. Asthma makes everyone feel out of control, and parents do not like feeling so helpless. Believe me, I know. I'm a parent.

Besides, I was raised by two very protective parents. I felt inadequate when they intervened in my life all the time. I thought that meant I was too stupid to know how to take care of myself. But I didn't know how to tell them that. It's ironic really. The best thing a parent can give a child is **independence**. But the overprotective parent makes his child **dependent**. You have the right to tell them how it makes you feel. (Nonetheless, don't gripe if you don't behave responsibly. Maybe you do need some supervision.)

3. **If you think your family is being torn apart by your asthma, involve them in your treatments.** Let them know your medication regimen; have one of them learn how to do postural drainage, if you need it. Once people are brought into another's experience, they often understand it better. If you're ever hospitalized, let all family members visit. Even very young brothers and sisters, if possible. Make sure everyone knows what's wrong and the purpose of the treatments. The more they understand, the more supportive they're likely to be.

4. **Keep as physically fit as possible.** The more fit you are, the less medication you may need. The stronger your heart and lungs, the fewer should be your complications. And more important, the more active you are, the higher your self-esteem. Although my young friend the aerobics instructor says her asthma seems to worsen as she ages, she still feels she has more control over it because she stays physically fit.

Along with being as physically fit as possible, learn to relax, too. When you're stressed, your muscles constrict. If you can learn to relax them, you'll be helping your bronchial tubes as well. They're made of muscle, too, and while you can't will them to dilate, you can relax and help the medication do the job.

5. **Manage your fear and anxiety by being prepared.** Keep your prescriptions filled and a second inhaler on hand when you've used half of the first one. You never know when your inhaler is actually empty—until it is— and you sure don't want to be caught short in the middle of an asthma attack. If you have food allergies or are allergic to bee stings, keep adrenaline around. When you travel, take all your medicines with you, even the "as needed" ones. You can't always predict your environment. What you don't react to **here** may set you off **there**. Always know the name of the nearest hospital and how to get there. Be responsive to your symptoms when they first appear; the complications will be fewer. The more you take control of the situation, the less anxiety you should feel.

And the more you keep your asthma under control, the less stress on the rest of your family. Asthma doesn't affect just individuals; it affects **families**.

Serious Family Problems

One other thing: If your asthma is complicated by severe family problems, you may need to do more than simply talk out your feelings. While asthma is a physical problem that **precedes** psychological problems, it will be worsened by family stress. If you have a dysfunctional family (one where there's a lot of fighting, misunderstandings and/or trauma), you need professional intervention. Again, talk to your doctor first. She can recommend affordable family therapy for you. Doctors have learned that it's more effective to treat the **whole family** rather than just the asthmatic. If your family members balk at being involved, let the professional decide how to handle it from there. The point is that your asthma won't significantly improve if family relations remain seriously troubled. One thing affects the other.

CHAPTER 15

Complications of

Asthma

NONCOMPLIANCE

The biggest cause of emergency-room visits and out-of-control asthma is patient noncompliance. People simply stop taking their medicine as prescribed by their doctor, or they fail to seek medical help in the first place. Maybe some of these people don't want to see themselves as being "sick." Maybe some can't afford all their prescriptions (and asthma medication does get very expensive). Then too, maybe some people think they're doing fine and no longer need any medicine.

One woman friend wrote me, "Sometimes I think the medicine isn't necessary. But when I skip, the asthma symptoms do return. So the secret is being regular in treatment."

Sometimes it's not that you intentionally disregard your medication regimen; you simply haven't understood it from your doctor. For example, the friend I just mentioned is supposed to use two different inhalers each day. Her doctor didn't initially explain to her that she needed to use them **together** (in conjunction with each other) to get the desired effect. Likewise, Michal uses an inhaler as needed before and during exercising, but she was told to use a special nasal spray routinely twice a day. Her doctor never told her that it was a cortisone spray. She merely said Michal would need to keep using it for a few weeks before she'd see much effect. Initially, Michal used the spray twice a day, but it got easier and easier to forget to use regularly. As I began working on this book, I realized her nasal spray was a cortisone derivative that she needed to use regularly as prescribed. Michal has been more compliant with treatment since the importance has been explained to her.

If you're noncompliant with your treatment regimen because you just don't care, I can only say that you're creating more complications for your asthma. If you're noncompliant because you don't understand what you're supposed to be doing (or how often a day you're supposed to be doing it), call your doctor (or nurse) immediately. Don't be embarrassed to ask why you're taking something. Don't be afraid to ask them to show you how to use it. And if you don't know what certain words mean in the directions, don't be afraid to ask. It's hard to be compliant when you don't understand the game plan. Doctors want you to follow their plans, as it makes for fewer problems. So they won't mind a bunch of questions if it engenders your cooperation in the long run.

ASTHMA AND SEX

I'm assuming you're either married or in a monogamous relationship and practicing safe sex. Moral issues aside, the rise and seriousness of sexually transmitted diseases, including AIDS, make casual sexual relationships a tremendous risk these days.

Sex is like exercise, and as such it can trigger asthma attacks. Your heart is beating harder; your breathing comes faster; and not surprisingly, your bronchial tubes constrict, just as if you were running the mile.

Even if exercise doesn't usually trigger an asthma attack, allergies to certain colognes might. Or simply worrying that you might start wheezing during an intimate moment . . .

First of all, rest assured that not all asthmatics have attacks during sex. In fact, probably most don't. Nonetheless, you can take certain precautions to lessen the likelihood of an attack. If exercising is a trigger for you, use your inhaler before sex just as you would before exercising. That sounds both unromantic and disruptive, but it doesn't have to be. If you know you'll be having sex, go use your inhaler (just as you would take a few minutes to insert a diaphragm). Just remember that it takes fifteen minutes for the medication to start working. Don't wait to use the inhaler at the last minute. If you plan a night of lovemaking, remember, too, that your medication only protects you for three to four hours. If it's been longer than that, you need to use your inhaler again.

Make sure your partner knows about your asthma condition. If you're allergic to strong colognes or perfumes, make sure he or she knows not to be wearing any. Make sure of your sleeping environment before you test for a reaction. Feather pillows might provoke a bronchospasm; houseplants in the bedroom might set you off.

If you're married to your partner, he or she undoubtedly knows you're asthmatic. If you're dating, and you're afraid that telling your partner you have asthma will turn him off, reconsider this sexual relationship. Sex is for intimates.

If you're going to have sex (aside from protecting against pregnancy), follow these steps for fewer complications.

1. Premedicate with an inhaler.
2. Consider a position where the asthmatic won't have undue pressure on his or her chest.
3. Slow down and forget about your performance. Worrying about having an attack will only stress you and increase the likelihood of having an attack. If you DO have an attack, simply stop and restore your breathing.
4. Asthma per se does not make you impotent, but some medications can have a dampening effect on your desire or ability. If you think that's a problem for you, consult your doctor. Surely he'll realize that if the medicine interferes with your sex life you're probably going to be less compliant with treatment. Maybe there's another medicine you can use instead. But you won't know unless you ask.

ASTHMA AND PREGNANCY

If you're worried that you won't ever be able to have children because you're an asthmatic, you can stop worrying. Lots of asthmatics give birth every year, and to perfectly healthy babies. If you're a teenager, I suggest postponing your pregnancy until you're financially and emotionally prepared for a baby. Babies are far more demanding than you can ever imagine, and not nearly as much fun in the beginning as everyone predicts.

But if you plan on conceiving in the future, rest assured

that only one third of all asthmatics get worse during pregnancy. The other two thirds are evenly divided between those whose asthma symptoms improve and those whose stay the same. And no one can predict which third you're likely to fall into. It's liable to vary with each pregnancy. Whatever happens in your case, after delivery your asthma will probably be the same as it was before pregnancy.

Discuss with your doctor your desire to get pregnant. You should be exploring your options well before you've had the decisions made for you. If you use an obstetrician, make sure he or she knows about your asthma and talks with your regular doctor. You may need to alter your medication regimen, and that is not something you do on your own.

First of all, you have nothing to worry about if you're the asthmatic father. No matter what medication you take even at the time of conception, it won't affect the fetus. Whether or not you'll pass on your asthma (genetically) to your child is something over which you have no control.

If you're the one wanting to get pregnant, and you have asthma, you'll want to be in as good physical shape as possible before conceiving. If possible, you and your doctor should try to have you get by with as little medication as you safely can. The first three months of pregnancy are the most dangerous because the fetus is forming—not just growing bigger. It's in this formative stage that medication can have its most profound effects. Doctors suggest using as little medicine during the first three months as possible because **everything** crosses the placenta. Any body part not properly developed in these first three months will not get a second chance. They either develop properly at that time or **not at all**.

Nonetheless, if you need medication to prevent an

asthma attack, you can't simply go without. An asthma attack, with its subsequent decrease in oxygen for both mother and fetus, is more dangerous than the medication's potential side effects. Pregnancy makes great demands on the woman's heart and lungs. Asthmatics who are pregnant are already stressed because of their own breathing difficulties. They hyperventilate more readily during pregnancy, and the growing fetus will push relentlessly against their diaphragm. If you suffer an asthma attack on top of this, your baby will lose oxygen the same as you. The results can be devastating.

So while medication should be kept to a minimum, and certain kinds avoided, all must be done to control the pregnant woman's asthma symptoms. Theophylline is reportedly the safest asthma medication to use after the first three months of pregnancy. Not only does it not have any documented teratogenic effects (causing fetus malformations), but it increases blood flow to the uterus.

Cromolyn is reportedly safe as a second line of defense, and bronchodilating inhalers probably have fewer side effects because they're inhaled. However, you need to talk over with your regular doctor which medication he or she thinks will be least harmful to your baby.

Adrenaline is the only asthma medication you **should not take during pregnancy**. Unless, of course, **your life is in danger**. If you need adrenaline to counter the effects of a severe asthma attack, obviously the side effects are going to be less dangerous than the attack. You see, adrenaline constricts blood vessels at the same time it dilates bronchial tubes. Constricting blood vessels reduces blood flow (and oxyen) to the uterus and placenta.

The bottom line is this: An asthma attack that reduces oxygen intake is far worse for the developing fetus than the medication used to prevent asthma symptoms. Don't ignore signs of an asthma attack and further endanger your baby's health by skipping medicine.

Rising hormones during pregnancy help some asthmatics better control their asthma symptoms. Progesterone aids in relaxing smooth muscle, which means it affects the muscle surrounding the bronchial tubes, too. Studies show that the most asthma complications occur between weeks twenty-four and thirty-six of a normally forty-week pregnancy. Fortunately, things clear up before labor and delivery. Only a very small number of asthmatics have symptoms during delivery.

Speaking of labor, here are some preventive things you can do. Practice relaxation techniques that will help lessen your anxiety. Tense muscles make for a harder labor. And make sure all your health-care workers (doctor, nurses, anesthesiologist) know you have asthma. Keep the inhaler with you during labor, though chances are you won't have to use it.

Other Medications During Pregnancy

Other medications to avoid during pregnancy are Vistaril, aspirin, sulfa drugs, and tetracycline. If you have headaches, use acetaminophen products in place of aspirin, especially in your last trimester.

If you've been taking allergy shots and having good results, it's safe to continue them during pregnancy. However, pregnancy is not a good time to initiate these shots. Wait until after you've had the baby to start shots. The last thing you need during pregnancy is an unexpected allergic reaction.

ASTHMA AND BREAST-FEEDING

Once you've had your baby and plan to breast-feed, the medications thought safest during pregnancy are not safest for breast-feeding. All ingested medicines will be in your breast milk. For that reason, theophylline is not a good choice because it has a tendency to make the baby jittery and nervous.

On the other hand, the beta-2-stimulating bronchodilators that you inhale are safest. That's because you're inhaling the medication, and it doesn't go through your system the way pills do.

What's the likelihood of your having an asthmatic child? Unfortunately the odds increase greatly if both you and the father have asthma and/or allergies. But there's nothing you can do (at least at this point in time) to prevent passing on the asthma gene, so you might as well relax. Breast-feeding a baby who might develop asthma supposedly can delay the asthma and allergy symptoms. Besides, you're living proof that asthma is treatable. We may not know how to cure asthma, but we can control it. In your baby's generation, the asthma gene may be isolated and a cure found. Scientists are working on it now.

ASTHMA AND DENTAL SURGERY

If you're facing dental surgery, or any kind of surgery, be sure to remind your dentist or doctor you have asthma. If you're taking corticosteroids, you'll need extra steroids because your body has temporarily lost its ability to produce additional cortisone. And you need that to recover from surgery.

Likewise, you don't want to undergo anesthesia without

the anesthesiologist knowing you're subject to asthma attacks. Anything that'll depress your respiration is dangerous.

ASTHMA AND PULMONARY INFECTIONS

The asthmatic is more susceptible to pulmonary infections. And any infection that might be short-lived in the average individual becomes a complication for the person with asthma. You can't live in isolation for fear of catching an infection, but you can be more attentive to signs of illness. Contact your doctor if you get a cold or other infection because you may need additional asthma medicine. If you're responsive to signs of respiratory illness, you'll encounter fewer complications with your asthma.

A FINAL WORD . . .

Asthma is a lifelong condition, unfortunately. While symptoms may abate for years, they may return in later age. If your asthma hasn't flared up for a while, don't worry about the day it may return. Enjoy your health, and if and when asthma symptoms return, you already know they're treatable. Contact your doctor and decide on a treatment regimen. In the meantime, let's hope a cure for asthma is just around the corner . . .

Appendix

MEDICATIONS UNDER CONSIDERATION

Ketotifen is the first oral antiasthma drug intended for prevention of asthma symptoms. It acts like cromolyn but is not inhaled. It's not currently available in the U.S., though it's being used elsewhere.

Back in the 1950s, the liberal use of the drug thalidomide during pregnancy led to a generation of babies born without limbs or with malformed limbs. Since that time, the FDA has clamped down on testing requirements new drugs have to meet. Before a new drug can be marketed, it has to pass five years of clinical testing. Albuterol (Proventil and Ventolin) was available in Europe and Canada for ten years before being approved in the United States. Cromolyn has been available in the U.S. since 1975, but got off to a slow start because doctors were so reluctant to switch over.

Other Drugs and Strategies

Tilade (nedocromil sodium) is awaiting FDA approval. It reportedly is more effective than cromolyn and is available in both the inhaler (MDI) and nebulizing liquid.

Three new long-acting beta-2-agonists are being developed. As you know, current inhalers provide relief for only three to four hours. These newer inhalers will have a twelve-hour effectiveness. **Formoterol** is reportedly ten times more potent than albuterol and has a rapid onset of action. (As it is now, you have to wait about fifteen minutes before your inhaler starts to relieve symptoms.) Formoterol is currently being used in Europe and Canada.

And lastly, scientists are working to isolate an asthma gene. Once they can isolate it, there is hope they can correct it by using altered gene therapy. And **that** represents a cure for asthma.

RESOURCES

Lung-Line in Denver will answer any of your questions about asthma. It is staffed between 8:30 and 5:00 pm, Monday through Friday. Messages are taken at other times and the calls returned.

The National Jewish Center for Immunology and Respiratory Medicine
    1–800–222–LUNG
        or, in Colorado: 1–303–398–1477.
(You do not have to be Jewish to use their services. The calls are free.)

Allergy and Asthma Network
3554 Chain Bridge Road
Fairfax, VA 22030–2709

American Academy of Allergy and Immunology
611 East Wells Street
Milwaukee, WI 53202–3889
    (This organization offers the *Asthma and Allergy Advocate* newsletter, plus numerous public education materials for a small fee.)

Patient's Guide to Asthma by Fred Leffert.
    This is a free booklet from Glaxo, Inc., 5 Moore Drive, Research Triangle Park, NC 27709

The Asthma and Allergy Foundation of America (AAFA)
1125 15th Street NW
Washington, DC 20005

This organization provides excellent resources, but it may take three to four weeks to receive the materials.

American Lung Association
1740 Broadway
New York, NY 10019

(This is another excellent resource. It will give you the address of your local American Lung Association chapter. It also provides an abundance of excellent materials free of charge.)

Glossary

aerosol A spray.

airway hyperreactivity Airways that are easily irritated or provoked to spasm.

allergens Substances that cause an allergic reaction.

alveoli (air sacs) Smallest parts of lungs where exchange of oxygen and carbon dioxide takes place.

anaphylaxis Most severe form of allergic reaction. The throat closes up and the victim dies without immediate intervention.

antihistamine Medication that counteracts the effects of the chemical histamine in the nasal passages.

arterial blood gases Test done on arterial blood to determine the level of oxygen and carbon dioxide.

bronchi Larger airways.

bronchoconstriction Closing off of airways.

bronchodilators drugs, such as albuterol (Proventil or Ventolin) that affect beta-2-receptors to open up the airways.

cilia Hairlike structures in the airways that allow mucus to be pushed along.

dyspnea Shortness of breath.

eosinophils White blood cells drawn to the site of mast cell explosion that will indicate an allergic reaction.

hives Allergic skin reaction (raised red blisters or spots).

hyperventilation Rapid, shallow breathing, leading to tingling sensation and oxygen deprivation.

hypoxia Inadequate oxygen in the body tissues.

immunotherapy Treatment of allergies (desensitization) by shots.

pulmonary disease Disease of the lungs, such as bronchitis or emphysema.

134

respiratory tract Airways from nose to mouth, down the trachea and including alveoli in lungs.

sputum Phlegm (mucus) coughed up from lungs.

status asthmaticus Life-threatening asthma attack.

teratogen Something that can cause malformations in developing fetuses.

trachea Windpipe or large airway.

For Further Reading

Haas, Drs. Francois and Sheila Sperber. *The Essential Asthma Book*. New York: Charles Scribner's Sons, 1987.

Hannaway, Paul. *The Asthma Self-Help Book*. Rocklin, CA: Prima Publishing, 1992.

Paul, Glennon H., and Fufoglia, Barbara. *All About Asthma and How to Live with It*. New York: Sterling Pub. Co, Inc., 1988.

Subak-Sharp, Genell. *Breathing Easy. A Handbook for Asthmatics*. New York: Doubleday. 1988.

Weinstein, Allan. *Asthma*. New York: McGraw-Hill Book Co., 1987.

Young, Stuart H. With Susan Shulman and Martin Shulman. *The Asthma Handbook (A Complete Guide For Patients and Their Families)*. New York: Bantam Books, 1989.

Index